First World War
and Army of Occupation
War Diary
France, Belgium and Germany

1 INDIAN CAVALRY DIVISION
Lucknow Cavalry Brigade
'U' Battery Royal Horse Artillery
31 August 1914 - 31 December 1916

WO95/1175/1

The Naval & Military Press Ltd
www.nmarchive.com
Published in association with The National Archives

Published by

The Naval & Military Press Ltd

Unit 10 Ridgewood Industrial Park,
Uckfield, East Sussex,
TN22 5QE England
Tel: +44 (0) 1825 749494

www.naval-military-press.com
www.nmarchive.com

This diary has been reprinted in facsimile from the original. Any imperfections are inevitably reproduced and the quality may fall short of modern type and cartographic standards.

Contents

Document type	Place/Title	Date From	Date To
Heading	WO95/1175/1		
Heading	##		
Heading	B.E.F. 1 Ind. Cav. Div. Lucknow Bde. "U" Bty. R.H.A. 1914 Aug to 1916 Dec		
Heading	War Diary of "U" Battery Royal Horse Artillery From 31st August 1914 to 25th December 1914.		
War Diary	Lucknow	31/08/1914	09/10/1914
War Diary	Bombay	09/10/1914	16/10/1914
War Diary	At Sea.	19/10/1914	23/10/1914
War Diary	Aden	24/10/1914	24/10/1914
War Diary	At Sea	24/10/1914	30/10/1914
War Diary	Port Said	30/10/1914	01/11/1914
War Diary	At Sea	01/11/1914	01/11/1914
War Diary	Marseilles	07/11/1914	10/11/1914
War Diary	Orleans	12/11/1914	07/12/1914
War Diary	Lillers	09/12/1914	22/12/1914
War Diary	Norrent Fontes.	22/12/1914	25/12/1914
War Diary	Henchim	25/12/1914	25/12/1914
War Diary	War Diary of "U" "M" Battery R.H.A. From 1st January 1915 To 31st January 1915		
War Diary	Henchim	12/01/1915	30/01/1915
Heading	Norrent Fontes	31/01/1915	31/01/1915
War Diary	War Diary of "U" Battery R.H.A. From 1st February 1915 To 26th February 1915		
War Diary		01/02/1915	26/02/1915
Heading	War Diary of "U" Battery R.H.A. From 1st March 1915 to 31st March 1915		
War Diary		04/03/1915	31/03/1915
Heading	War Diary of "U" Battery R.F.A. From 1st April 1915 To 30th April 1915		
War Diary		01/04/1915	30/04/1915
Heading	War Diary of "U" Battery R.H.A. From 1st May 1915 To 31st May 1915		
War Diary		01/05/1915	31/05/1915
War Diary	War Diary of "U" Battery R.H.A. From 1st June 1915 To 30th June 1915		
War Diary		01/06/1915	30/06/1915
Heading	War Diary of "U" Battery R.H.A. From 1st July 1915 To 31st July 1915		
War Diary		01/07/1915	31/07/1915
Heading	War Diary of "U" Battery R.H.A. From 1st August 1915 To 31st August 1915		
War Diary		01/08/1915	31/08/1915
Heading	War Diary of "U" Battery Royal Horse Artillery From 1st September 1915 To 30th November 1915		
War Diary	Duzanne.	01/09/1915	30/09/1915
War Diary	Field.	01/10/1915	31/10/1915
War Diary	Fourdrenoy	01/11/1915	30/11/1915
War Diary	War Diary of "U" Battery Royal Horse Artillery From 1st December 1915 To 31st December 1915		

War Diary	Metigny-Laleu	01/12/1915	31/12/1915
War Diary	Lavieville	18/12/1915	31/12/1915
Heading	War Diary of "U" Battery Royal Horse Artillery From 1st January 1916 To 31st January 1916		
War Diary	Lavieville	01/01/1916	31/01/1916
Heading	War Diary of "U" Battery Royal Horse Artillery From 1st February 1916 To 29th February 1916		
War Diary	Lavieville	03/02/1916	05/02/1916
War Diary	Ochancourt	07/02/1916	29/02/1916
Heading	War Diary of "U" Battery Royal Horse Artillery From 1st March 1916 To 31st March 1916		
War Diary	Ochancourt	02/03/1916	31/03/1916
Heading	War Diary of "U" Battery Royal Horse Artillery From 1st April 1916 To 30 April 1916		
War Diary	Tollent	01/04/1916	30/04/1916
Heading	War Diary of "U" Battery Royal Horse Artillery From 1st May 1916 To 31st May 1916.		
War Diary	Agenvillers	01/05/1916	31/05/1916
Heading	War Diary of "U" Battery Royal Horse Artillery From 1st June 1916 To 30th June 1916		
War Diary	F 11. A 37 Near Mt St Eloy.	01/06/1916	30/06/1916
War Diary	War Diary of "U" Battery Royal Horse Artillery From 1st July 1916 To 31st July 1916		
War Diary	Doullens	01/07/1916	31/07/1916
War Diary		01/08/1916	10/08/1916
War Diary	Montauban	11/08/1916	27/08/1916
War Diary	?	28/08/1916	29/08/1916
War Diary	N. of ?	30/08/1916	30/08/1916
War Diary	? Wood	30/08/1916	30/08/1916
Heading	War Diary of "U" Battery Royal Horse Artillery From 1st September 1916 To 30th September 1916		
War Diary	N of Bernafay Wood.	01/09/1916	05/09/1916
War Diary	Becordel.	05/09/1916	05/09/1916
War Diary	La Neuville.	05/09/1916	15/09/1916
War Diary	Ville-sur-Ancre	15/09/1916	25/09/1916
War Diary	Mametz	25/09/1916	25/09/1916
War Diary	Ville-sur-Ancre	26/09/1916	26/09/1916
War Diary	Mametz.	26/09/1916	27/09/1916
War Diary	Ville-sur-Ancre	27/09/1916	27/09/1916
War Diary	Buissy.	27/09/1916	28/09/1916
War Diary	Crouy	28/09/1916	29/09/1916
War Diary	Eaucourt.	29/09/1916	30/09/1916
War Diary	Rossignol	30/09/1916	30/09/1916
War Diary	War Diary of "U" Battery Royal Horse Artillery From 1st October 1916 To 30th November 1916		
War Diary		01/10/1916	01/10/1916
War Diary	Rosignol	01/10/1916	01/10/1916
War Diary	Crecy.	02/10/1916	19/10/1916
War Diary	Neux	20/10/1916	20/10/1916
War Diary	Havernas.	21/10/1916	22/10/1916
War Diary	Crecy.	23/10/1916	02/11/1916
War Diary	Moyenneville	03/11/1916	19/11/1916
War Diary	L'Etoile	20/11/1916	20/11/1916
War Diary	Vaux-En-Amienois	21/11/1916	23/11/1916
War Diary	Vaux.	24/11/1916	30/11/1916

Heading	War Diary of "U" Battery Royal Horse Artillery From 1st December 1916 To 31st December 1916		
War Diary	Vaux-En-Amienois	01/12/1916	31/12/1916

WO 95/1175/1

B.E.F. FRANCE & FLANDERS.

INDIAN CAV DIVISION.

LUCKNOW BRIGADE.

'U' BTY ROYAL HORSE ARTY

1914 AUG TO 1916 DEC.

'G' AMMN COLUMN R.H.A.

1914 AUG TO 1915 MAR.

BRIGADE SIGNAL TROOP.

1914 AUG TO 1916 DEC.

MACHINE GUN SQUADRON.

1916 JAN TO 1916 DEC.

BDE SUPPLY OFFICER.

1914 AUG TO 1916 SEPT.

BDE TRANSPORT OFFICER.

1914 NOV TO 1915 JULY.

1916 JULY TO 1916 SEPT.

MOBILE VETERINARY SECTION

1914 NOV TO 1916 DEC.

1125

B.E.F.FRANCE & FLANDERS

1 INDIAN CAV DIVISION.

LUCKNOW BRIGADE.

'U' BTY ROYAL HORSE AR

1914 AUG TO 1916 DEC.

'G' AMMN COLUMN R.H.A.

1914 AUG TO 1915 MAR.

BRIGADE SIGNAL TROOP.

1914 AUG TO 1916 DEC.

MACHINE GUN SQUADRON.

1916 JAN TO 1916 DEC.

BDE SUPPLY OFFICER.

1914 AUG TO 1916 SEPT.

BDE TRANSPORT OFFICER.

1914 NOV TO 1915 JULY.

1916 JULY TO 1916 SEPT

MOBILE VETERINARY SECT

1914 NOV TO 1916 DEC.

1175

B.E.F.

1 IND. CAV. DIV.

LUCKNOW BDE.

"U" BTY. R.H.A.

1914 AUG to 1916 DEC

E2

W A R D I A R Y

of

"U" Battery Royal Horse Artillery

from 31st August1914 to 25th December 1914.

Instructions regarding War Diaries and Intelligence Summaries are contained in F. S. Regs., Part II, and the Staff Manual respectively. Title pages will be prepared in manuscript.

WAR DIARY

or

~~INTELLIGENCE SUMMARY.~~

(Erase heading not required.)

Army Form C. 2118.

Hour, Date, Place.	Summary of Events and Information.	Remarks and references to Appendices
Lucknow		
10.30 am 31-8-14	Received orders to mobilize	
11 am 11-9-14	Reported mobilization complete with the exception of Horses.	
12.30 am 13th Sept 1914	Reported mobilization complete	
6 am 4th Oct	Right half Battery entrained for Bombay	
9.50 am 4th Oct	Left half Battery entrained for Bombay	
Bombay		
6 am } 9.30 am } 9th Oct	Battery de-trained were encamped on the Marine Lines	
8 am 13th Oct	Battery embarked on SS Ballarat at Alexandra Docks.	
5 pm 16th Oct	Battery sailed.	
At Sea		
19th Oct	Gunr Battery No 88 died	

Army Form C. 2118.

Instructions regarding War Diaries and Intelligence Summaries are contained in F. S. Regs., Part II, and the Staff Manual respectively. Title pages will be prepared in manuscript.

WAR DIARY

~~or~~

~~INTELLIGENCE SUMMARY.~~

(*Erase heading not required.*)

Hour, Date, Place.	Summary of Events and Information.	Remarks and references to Appendices
At Sea		
21st Oct	Horses Battery No 39 + 33 died	
22nd Oct	Horses Battery No 214 died	
23rd Oct	Horse Battery No 191 died	
Aden		
2 am 24th Oct	Arrived at Aden	
~~6 am 24th Oct~~	~~Left Aden~~	
6 am 24th Oct	No 40669 Driver Davies R & No 47549 Driver Lovett C disembarked as sick patients	
6.30am 24th Oct	Left Aden	
At Sea		
26th Oct	Horse Bty No 192 died	
27th Oct	Horse Bty No 211 died	
29th Oct	Horse Bty No 134 died	
6pm 29th Oct	Arrived at Port Suez	
7am 30th Oct	Left Port Suez	

Army Form C. 2118.

WAR DIARY

~~INTELLIGENCE SUMMARY.~~

(*Erase heading not required.*)

Instructions regarding War Diaries and Intelligence Summaries are contained in F. S. Regs., Part II, and the Staff Manual respectively. Title pages will be prepared in manuscript.

Hour, Date, Place.	Summary of Events and Information.	Remarks and references to Appendices
Port Said		
8pm 30th Oct	Arrived at Port Said	
10am 31st Oct	No 44177 Gunner J. McDonald & No 49435 Gunner Cope R.G.A. dis-embarked as sick [illegible]	
11am 1st Nov	Left Port Said	
At Sea		
4pm 1st Nov	Charger of Lt Col Rolleston destroyed [illegible]	
Marseilles		
6am 9th Nov	Arrived at Marseilles	
8am 9th Nov	Battery dis-embarked & camped on the quay for the night.	
11am 9th Nov	Battery proceeded to St Valentine Camp.	
10th Nov.	2Lt. J Kahane joined Battery as Intrepreter	
1pm 10th Nov	Left camp & entrained for Orleans.	
Orleans		
4.30pm 12th Nov	Battery de-trained & proceeded to La Source Camp	

Instructions regarding War Diaries and Intelligence Summaries are contained in F. S. Regs., Part II, and the Staff Manual respectively. Title pages will be prepared in manuscript.

WAR DIARY

or

~~INTELLIGENCE SUMMARY.~~

(Erase heading not required.)

Army Form C. 2118.

Hour, Date, Place.	Summary of Events and Information.	Remarks and references to Appendices
Orleans		
5.55 pm 4th DEC.	Battery entrained for Lillers.	
Lillers.		
6 am 9th DEC.	Battery de-trained & proceeded to Billets	
4.50 pm 21st DEC.	2/Lt J. Kaffane left Bty under orders of A.G.	
5.30 am 22nd DEC.	Battery left & proceeded by road to Norres Fontes	
~~[illegible]~~ Norres Fontes.		
8 am 22nd DEC.	Battery arrived & proceeded to Billets.	
9 am 25th DEC.	Battery left & proceeded by road to Henchin	
Henchin		
2.30 pm 25th DEC.	Battery arrived & proceeded to Billets.	R. Lascelles Major R.H.A. Comd E.M. Battery R.H.A.
~~[illegible] DEC.~~	~~Major H. Denniston left Battery for England [illegible]~~	
~~[illegible]~~	~~[illegible] left Battery on posting to 11th Div.~~	

WAR DIARY

OF

"U" "N" Battery R. H. A.

From 11th January 1915 To 31st January 1915

Army Form C. 2118.

Instructions regarding War Diaries and Intelligence Summaries are contained in F. S. Regs., Part II, and the Staff Manual respectively. Title pages will be prepared in manuscript.

WAR DIARY
or
INTELLIGENCE SUMMARY.

(*Erase heading not required.*)

Hour, Date, Place.	Summary of Events and Information.	Remarks and references to Appendices
Merchin 5.30 pm 12th January 1915	Major J.G. Dennistoun left Battery on posting to Home Establishment.	
10 am 11th Jan. 1915	Captain C.B. Findlay left Battery on posting to 1st Division.	
15th January 1915	Lieut P.E. Inchbald joined Battery from 15th Bty R.F.A.	
15th January 1915	2/Lt E.C.B. Dale joined Battery from 112th Bty R.F.A.	
16th January 1915	Major R.H. Lascelles joined Battery from "Q" Bty RHA & assumed command.	
16th January 1915	2/Lt H.W. Huggins joined Battery from 44th Bty R.F.A.	
17th January 1915	Left Battery on posting to Home Establishment (Capt H.K. Fournall)	
11 am 30th January 1915	Battery left Merchin & proceeded by road to Norrent Fontes & went into Billets for the night.	
Norrent Fontes 9.30 am 31st January 1915	Battery left Norrent Fontes & proceeded by road to [illegible] arriving about 3.30 pm where it went into Billets	R Lascelles

Serial No. 273.

121/5114

WAR DIARY

OF

"U." Battery R.H.A.

From 1st February 1915 To 26th February 1915

"U" By RHA

Army Form C. 2118.

WAR DIARY
or
INTELLIGENCE SUMMARY.

(*Erase heading not required.*)

Instructions regarding War Diaries and Intelligence Summaries are contained in F. S. Regs., Part II, and the Staff Manual respectively. Title pages will be prepared in manuscript.

Hour, Date, Place.	Summary of Events and Information.	Remarks and references to Appendices
1915		
Feby. 1st.	Marched to billets near Vlamertinghe. Centre Section moved on after dark into a position about 600 yds. W. of Hooge, and dug itself in. A bad position and a good deal shelled. B. S. M. Brooks joined battery on posting, also the following drivers:- Baker, Davies, Jewett, Newman, Simms, Blowe Rowe, and Tanner, on the night of the 31st Jany. 1915.	
Feby 2nd.	Right Section moved after dark into a position near level crossing, about 800 yds. N.W. of Hooge. Centre Section registered in morning. Left Section moved to position in left rear of Right Section, to act against aircraft.	
Feby. 3rd.	Digging in all day. Centre Section moved alongside Right Section after dark. Left Section fired nearly 100 rounds at aeroplanes. Registered again. Fired about 40 rounds at night as there was a lot of rifle fire going on.	
Feby 4th & 5th.	Nothing to report.	
Feby 6th.	Got orders from C. R. A. to move to a new position, S. of YPRES-MENIN road. Selected one about 600 yds. S.W. of Hooge and moved Right & Centre Sections after dark, sending Left Section to billets. Got in without casualty.	
Feby 7th.	A few 77 m. m. shell round about, they were mostly filled with marbles. Registered in morning. Gunner Ewing wounded.	

Instructions regarding War Diaries and Intelligence Summaries are contained in F. S. Regs., Part II, and the Staff Manual respectively. Title pages will be prepared in manuscript.

WAR DIARY

or

INTELLIGENCE SUMMARY.

(Erase heading not required.)

Army Form C. 2118.

Hour, Date, Place.	Summary of Events and Information.	Remarks and references to Appendices
1915		
Feby 8th & 9th.	Quiet days, varied by occasional shelling. Gr. Crowther wounded.	
Feby. 10th.	Right Section relieved by a Section of Belgian Artillery.	
Feby. 11th.	Remainder of Battery relieved by Belgian Artillery. Lieut. Inchbald left temporarily attached to 367th. Battery R.F.A. and 2/Lieut Stansfield was attached to "U" Battery. RHA	
Feby. 12th.	Marched to and billetted near Abeele.	
Feby 13th.	Marched to billets in Rely. The three batteries R.H.A. of 1st. Indian Cavalry Division being now centralised and made into Divisional Troops.	
Feby 23rd.	Four cast horses sent away.	
Feby 24th.	Four gunners arrived from Rouen	
Feby 26th.	Nine horses joined. 1 Horse destroyed	

R. Lascelles.

Are R.H.A. Batts but which?
C.W.
22/3/17

Serial No. 273

121/5114

WAR DIARY

OF

"U." Battery R. H. A.

From 4th March 1915 [illegible] 31st March 1915

1st

Instructions regarding War Diaries and Intelligence Summaries are contained in F. S. Regs., Part II, and the Staff Manual respectively. Title pages will be prepared in manuscript.

WAR DIARY
or
INTELLIGENCE SUMMARY.
(Erase heading not required.)

Army Form C. 2118.

Hour, Date, Place.		Summary of Events and Information.	Remarks and references to Appendices
1.30. a.m	4 3/15.	Battery marched from Billets in Rely, to Merville.	
7.30. a.m.	4 3/15	Battery arrived at Merville, + went into billets.	
6.15. p.m	4 3/15.	Battery left Merville. + took up a position at La Flinque	
	5 3/15	Battery started registering on enemy's positions	
	6-9 3/15.	Battery continued registering, on evening of 9th. teams brought up to Rue Paradis.	
7.30. a.m.	10 3/15	Battery took part in the bombardment of NEUVE CHAPELLE, and continued firing at intervals all day on various points behind German trenches.	
	11 3/15.	Bombardment of enemy's trenches, and fortified houses occupied by them. Engaged German infantry retiring about midday, and a German convoy at 5-15 p.m.	
	12 3/15.	Bombardment quietened down, and battery's fire mainly directed on enemy's trenches, + hostile artillery. We were ordered to protect our Infantry from possible counterattacks.	
	13 3/15	Quiet day. Gunners Parsons + Slingsby wounded.	
	14-16 3/15.	Nothing to report.	
	17 3/15	6 horses joined battery.	
	18 3/15.	Nothing to report.	
	19 3/15	Gunner Smith J. to hospital.	
	20-21 3/15	Nothing to report.	
	22 3/15	1 Horse to Divl. Ammn. Col. 1 horse to Mobile Vety. Section.	
	23 3/15	Nothing to report.	
	24 3/15	Battery registered on new points behind enemy's trenches.	
	25 3/15	Used 11 more rounds registering	
	26 3/15	Gunner Levett to hospital.	

Army Form C. 2118.

WAR DIARY

or

INTELLIGENCE SUMMARY.

(Erase heading not required.)

Instructions regarding War Diaries and Intelligence Summaries are contained in F. S. Regs., Part II, and the Staff Manual respectively. Title pages will be prepared in manuscript.

Hour, Date, Place.	Summary of Events and Information.	Remarks and references to Appendices
24 3/15.	Moved (w[r] line) billets to PONT RUCHIN, 2 miles in rear of gun position. Gunner Walsh to hospital. 1 horse to Mobile Vety. Section.	
28-29 3/15.	Nothing to report.	
30th. 3/15.	11 Gunners, 1 Farrier, + 1 Fitter joined battery.	
31 3/15	Dvr. Justin to Hospital.	

Field.
31st. Mar. 1915.

[signature] Lascelles.
Major, R. H. A
Commdg. "U" Bty. R. H. A

121/5504

Serial No. 273.

WAR DIARY

OF

"U" Battery R.F.A.

From 1st April 1915 To 30th April 1915

Instructions regarding War Diaries and Intelligence Summaries are contained in F. S. Regs., Part II, and the Staff Manual respectively. Title pages will be prepared in manuscript.

WAR DIARY
or
INTELLIGENCE SUMMARY.
(Erase heading not required.)

Army Form C. 2118.

Hour, Date, Place.	Summary of Events and Information.	Remarks and references to Appendices
April 1915.		
1st.	Nothing to report.	
2nd.	12021. Gnr. A. E. Jones, joined from Base.	
3rd.	3 Officers chargers joined.	
4th.	Nothing to report.	
5th.	Registered on a fresh line of German Trenches.	
6th.	Nothing to report.	
7th.	Battery vacated (temporarily) position at LA FLINQUE and marched into billets at MERVILLE.	
8th. 9th. 10th. + 11th.	Nothing to report.	
12th.	1 Light draught horse to Mobile Vety. Section. 24 Gunners attached from Divisional Ammunition Column, 1st. Indian Cavalry Division. 1 Light draught horse to Divisional Ammunition Column 1st. Indian Cavalry Division	
13th.	Nothing to report.	
14th.	Asst. Surgeon J. Courtney to hospital.	
15th.	Gunner Mitchell to hospital. 4 Mules, 2. Mule Carts and 2 Mule Drivers, to Divisional Transport Officer, 1st. Indian Cavalry Division.	
16th.	1 Riding and 2 Light draught horses to Mobile Vety. Section. Battery left MERVILLE to reoccupy position at LA FLINQUE.	
17th.	Battery registered for line.	
18th.	Ind. Dvr. Khushi Ram to hospital.	
19th.	Asst. Surgeon Ellmann, joined for duty.	
20th.	Nothing to report.	
21st.	2 Light draught horses to Mobile Vety Section. Left Section moved after dark into a new position at CROIX MARECHAL, with orders to prepare position for whole battery.	
22nd. + 23rd.	Battery fired six rounds at a German working party with successful results. Left Section registered on both days.	

Instructions regarding War Diaries and Intelligence Summaries are contained in F. S. Regs., Part II, and the Staff Manual respectively. Title pages will be prepared in manuscript.

WAR DIARY

or

INTELLIGENCE SUMMARY.

(Erase heading not required.)

Army Form C. 2118.

Hour, Date, Place.	Summary of Events and Information.	Remarks and references to Appendices
April 1915		
24th.	Registration continued by left Section. Dr. Jackson and Gunner Hughes to hospital. Battery fired twelve rounds at German trenches, as ours at the time was being heavily bombarded. Battery vacated position at LA FLINQUE, to rejoin 1st. Indian Cavalry Division as a four gun battery.	
25th.	Battery arrived and billetted at ST. SYLVESTRE-CAPELLE. Battery left ST. SYLVESTRE-CAPELLE, and marched into billets at MARIE-CAPELLE.	
26th.	Nothing to report.	
27th.	Nothing to report with the exception of the admission to hospital of Dvr. France, and the joining of one riding horse.	
28th.	Drs. Brown, A., to hospital. two light draught horses cast. Battery left MARIE-CAPELLE, and marched with 1st. Indian Cavalry Division into billets, at WATOU.	
29th.	Dvr. Ashton J., to hospital.	
30th.	Gnr. Patterson, A., transferred from Divisional Ammunition Column, 1st Indian Cavalry Division, for duty in battery.	
Field 2-5-15.	W. Maswelles. Major. RHA Commdg. "U" Bty. RHA	

121/5799

Serial No. 243.

Lucknow Bde

WAR DIARY

OF

"U." Battery R.H.A.

From 1st May 1915 To 31st May 1915.

Army Form C. 2118.

Instructions regarding War Diaries and Intelligence Summaries are contained in F. S. Regs., Part II, and the Staff Manual respectively. Title pages will be prepared in manuscript.

WAR DIARY

or

INTELLIGENCE SUMMARY.

(Erase heading not required.)

Hour, Date, Place.	Summary of Events and Information.	Remarks and references to Appendices
May 1915.		
1st.	2/Lt. Jeune, who had been acting as Interpreter to Battery, rejoined his unit 6th. Cavalry.	
2nd.	Battery left WATOU and marched into billets at MARIE-CAPELLE which place, in the evening the battery left. Sgts Hewart, Woodham, and Corpl. Gerrard joined Dvl. Ammn. Col. 1st. I. C. D., on promotion.	
3rd.	Battery arrived and billeted E. of SAILLY. In the evening the battery left this billet and went into a position at CROIX MARECHAL, the wagon line being at FLEURBAIX. Driver Ashton rejoined from hospital.	
4th.	Left Section rejoined, thus bringing battery up to full strength. Battery registered on enemy's positions both morning and afternoon. 2/Lieut. Harvey R.F.A. attached to battery for duty.	
5th	Battery continued registering. 2 Light draught horses to Mobile Veterinary Section. Br. Venables rejoined from Dvl Ammn. Col. 1st. I. C. D.	
6th	Drvs. Challen, Camp, Mulgrew, Peckham joined from Base.	
7th	Registration by battery brought to a conclusion.	
8th	Battery expecting action fired a couple of rounds to find error of the day. Ind. Dr. Khuda Bux to hospital.	
9th.	Battery took part with the 8th. Divisional Artillery in supporting infantry attacks	
10th.	Battery vacated position at CROIX MARECHAL. Cpl Brown, to hospital, also Dr. Lovatt.	
11th.	Battery arrived and went into billets at GORRE, and one section moved after dark, into a position 1000 yds W. of FESTUBERT.	

Army Form C. 2118.

Instructions regarding War Diaries and Intelligence Summaries are contained in F. S. Regs., Part II, and the Staff Manual respectively. Title pages will be prepared in manuscript.

WAR DIARY
or
INTELLIGENCE SUMMARY.

(Erase heading not required.)

Hour, Date, Place.	Summary of Events and Information.	Remarks and references to Appendices
May 1915		
12th.	Battery registered. Wagon line moved to near HAMEL. Remaining two sections came into position.	
13th.	Battery took part in bombardment of German trenches in the evening. 2/Lt. Stansfield rejoined 367th. Battery R.F.A. taking with him two chargers. Eight Light draught horses joined battery also on this date.	
14th.	Bombardment of enemy's trenches continued until early hours of morning. Bursts of fire kept up by battery at intervals all day and night. Lieut. R.E. Inchbald rejoined from 367th Battery RFA	
15th.	Battery again fired on German trenches. The Centre Section moved into position, in the British first line trench.	
16th.	Sergt. Campbell, to hospital having shrapnel wounds in scalp and leg. Firing all day of infantry attack. Silenced two hostile guns at 5.30 am, and they did not open fire again all day. Engaged three visible infantry targets.	
17th.	Fired at intervals throughout day. Mule Driver, Mule Cart and two mules to Divl. Ammn. Col. 1st. I.C.D. receiving in exchange British driver, 2 Light draught horses, and one G.S. wagon, limbered	
18th.	Battery again supported an infantry attack, Centre Section rejoined battery after dark.	
19th.	Battery fired on German trenches throughout day. Gnr. Jones, to hospital.	
20th.	Battery supported an infantry attack in the evening. 1 Light draught horse shot.	
21st.	Battery vacated position W. of FESTUBERT, and were shelled in so doing, by the enemy, who were searching and sweeping the country round about.	

Instructions regarding War Diaries and Intelligence Summaries are contained in F. S. Regs., Part II, and the Staff Manual respectively. Title pages will be prepared in manuscript.

WAR DIARY

or

INTELLIGENCE SUMMARY.

(Erase heading not required.)

Army Form C. 2118.

Hour, Date, Place.	Summary of Events and Information.	Remarks and references to Appendices
May 1915.		
22nd.	Battery arrived and went into billets at ROQUETOIRE. One Light draught horse shot. In afternoon battery lines were moved about a thousand yards farther on, to LIGNE	
23rd.	2/Lieut Harvey, R.F.A. left battery to return to England.	
24th	3 light draught horses to mobile Vety. Section. 3 Light draught horses to 1st. I.C.D.	
25th	Nothing to report.	
26th	4 light draught horses to mobile Vety Section. 4 light draught horses cast.	
27th	Battery left LIGNE and marched into billets near STAPLE.	
28th	Battery left STAPLE and marched into billets near RUBROUCH	
29th	Battery lines were shifted to a better farm close by.	
30th	Dr. Mulgrew, hospital.	
31st	1 Light draught horse to mobile Vety Section. Sgt Holmes to hospital	
Field 3-6-15	[signature] Major, RHA Comdg 'A' Battery RHA	

Serial No. 273.

121/6128

WAR DIARY

OF

"U" Battery R.H.A.

From 1st June 1915. To 30th June 1915.

Army Form C. 2118.

Instructions regarding War Diaries and Intelligence Summaries are contained in F. S. Regs., Part II, and the Staff Manual respectively. Title pages will be prepared in manuscript.

WAR DIARY

or

INTELLIGENCE SUMMARY.

(Erase heading not required.)

Hour, Date, Place.	Summary of Events and Information.	Remarks and references to Appendices
June 1915.		
1st + 2nd.	Nothing to report.	
3rd.	Gnr. Gurney to hospital	
4th.	Gnr. Ham, to hospital. Gr. Watson, rejoined from hospital.	
5th.	Sgt. Silvester, to hospital, 20 L.D. Horses joined	
6th.	2 L.D. horses to "A" Battery R.H.A. 1 L.D. horse to Signal Squadron, 1st. I.C.D.	
7th.	Nothing to report.	
8th.	Gnr. Honeybun, to hospital.	
9th.	Gnr. Springhall to hospital, Sgt. Silvester, rejoined from hospital, Br. Burgess, to hospital. 6 Drivers joined.	
10th.	Gr. Bradley to hospital, 11 L.D. horses cast, 2 L.D. horses to M.V.S. Gr. Gurney from hospital.	
11th.	Ind. Dr. Ghazi Khan, to hospital, 2 L.D. horses rejoined from M.V.S. Gr. Honeybun from hospital.	
12th.	Dr. Simms, to hospital. 1 L.D. horse to M.V.S. Gr. Curnock, to hospital.	
13th + 14th.	Nothing to report.	
15th.	Battery left billets and marched to ROQUETOIRE and billeted there.	

Army Form C. 2118.

WAR DIARY

or

INTELLIGENCE SUMMARY.

(Erase heading not required.)

Instructions regarding War Diaries and Intelligence Summaries are contained in F. S. Regs., Part II, and the Staff Manual respectively. Title pages will be prepared in manuscript.

Hour, Date, Place.	Summary of Events and Information.	Remarks and references to Appendices
June 1915		
16th.	Dr. France, rejoined Battery from "I" Battery RHA. Gr. Sills, to hospital. 7 Gunners joined.	
17th.	22 L.D. horses joined. Dr. Simms, rejoined from hospital	
18th.	Nothing to report.	
19th.	Gr. C. F. Sharp, & Gr. D. McGregor to hospital	
20th.	aBr. Harvey, to hospital.	
21st.	Nothing to report.	
22nd.	7 Gunners joined battery.	
23rd.	Nothing to report.	
24th.	Gunners attached, from 1st. I. C. D. A. C. rejoin their unit.	
25th.	Gnr. C. F. Sharp. from hospital	
26th.	Gnr. C. F. Sharp, to 1st. I. C. D. A. C.	
27th. 28th. 29th & 30th.	Nothing to report.	

Field.
5-7-15.

[signature]
Major, RHA.
Comdg "U" Battery RHA

Serial No. 273.

121/6502

WAR DIARY OF

"U." Battery R. H. A.

FROM 1st July 1915. To 31st July 1915

2

Army Form C. 2118.

Instructions regarding War Diaries and Intelligence Summaries are contained in F. S. Regs., Part II, and the Staff Manual respectively. Title page will be prepared in manuscript.

WAR DIARY
or
INTELLIGENCE SUMMARY.
(*Erase heading not required.*)

Hour, Date, Place.	Summary of Events and Information.	Remarks and references to Appendices
July 1915. 1st	Nothing to report.	
2nd	I. Driver Manga Khan joined.	
3rd	4 L. D. horses joined. Sjt. Wallis to hospital. Sjt. Strutter to Divl. Ammn. Col. 1st I. C. Div. Dr. Mitchell joined from "K" Battery. Dr. Englefield to "K" Battery in return	
4th	Nothing to report.	
5th	Sjt. Wallis from hospital.	
6th	Sjt. Child joined from Divl. Ammn. Col.	
	Gr. Suthers " " " "	
	Gr. Robinson J. to Divl. Ammn. Colm.	
7th	Nothing to report.	
8th	2 Heavy & 1 light D. horses to Mr. Vety. Sectn.	
9th	Nothing to report.	
10th	Battery moved from ROQUETOIRE & marched into billet at NIELLES. 8 L. D. horses joined.	

Instructions regarding War Diaries and Intelligence Summaries are contained in F. S. Regs., Part II, and the Staff Manual respectively. Title pages will be prepared in manuscript.

WAR DIARY

or

INTELLIGENCE SUMMARY.

(Erase heading not required.)

Army Form C. 2118.

Hour, Date, Place.	Summary of Events and Information.	Remarks and references to Appendices
July 1915		
11th	Nothing to report.	
12th	Inspection by G.O.C. Lucknow Cavalry Brigade.	
13th	Bdrs Churchill & Unwin go on "wireless course".	
14th	Nothing to report.	
15th	1 L.D. horse to Mobile Vety. Section.	
16th	Dr Snell to hospital	
17th	Nothing to report.	
18th	— Do —	
19th	4 L.D. horses sent to Divl. Ammn. Col. 11 L.D. " " " Remount Depôt.	
20th	Nothing to report.	
21st	Dr Smith A. to hospital.	
22nd	Nothing to report.	
23rd	— Do. —	
24th	Gr Brackenbury* & Cpl. Allen to K Battery. Cpl. Bywater from K Battery.	*claimed by elder brother.

Army Form C. 2118.

WAR DIARY

or

INTELLIGENCE SUMMARY.

(Erase heading not required.)

Instructions regarding War Diaries and Intelligence Summaries are contained in F. S. Regs., Part II, and the Staff Manual respectively. Title pages will be prepared in manuscript.

Hour, Date, Place.	Summary of Events and Information.	Remarks and references to Appendices
July 1915		
25th	Nothing to report	
26	—— do. ——	
27	Sgt Eldridge transferred to 87th Bde. R.F.A. 19th Division	
28	Nothing to report	
29	—— do ——	
30	—— do ——	
31st	Dr Crosbie & Gnr. Creighton to hospital.	
	Field 1st Aug st 1915	
	[illegible] Major R.H.A. Commanding U Battery RHA	

Serial No. 243.

121/6948

WAR DIARY

OF

"U" Battery R.H.A.

FROM 1st August 1915. To 31st August 1915

2

Army Form C. 2118.

Instructions regarding War Diaries and Intelligence Summaries are contained in F. S. Regs., Part II, and the Staff Manual respectively. Title pages will be prepared in manuscript.

WAR DIARY
or
INTELLIGENCE SUMMARY.

(*Erase heading not required.*)

Hour, Date, Place.		Summary of Events and Information.	Remarks and references to Appendices
August 1915	1.	Left NIELLES + marched to FRUGES. Gunner Duffy J. to Hospital.	
	2.	Left FRUGES + marched to AUBYN-St-VAAST.	
	3.	" AUBYN-St-VAAST + marched to BEAUMETZ.	
	4	" BEAUMETZ + marched to VAUCHELLES-L-Somme. Lt Inchbald, Gunner Hodgkins + Driver Bendall left for 5 Div. RFA.	
	5	1 horse to A Battery.	
	6	Gunner 53498 F.H. Graham apptd acty Fitter from 16-12-14.	
	7.	1 L.D Horse to Mobile Vet Section. Gr Creighton from Hospital. Lt Morrison joined + 1 Offrs charger.	
	8.	Indian Driver Wahil Deen to Hospital. No 99690 Dr Lowe F.R. joined. 3 "Q" Bty men attached till we meet "Q"	
	9.	39682 Gr Bullock H.J. to Hospital. 3 "Q" Bty men joined their own unit.	
	10.	Left VAUCHELLES + marched to St HILAIRE to a field having better water for the horses.	
	11	51152 Dr Crosbie J. to Hospital. 1 L.D. horse died.	
	12	88520 Dr Myers W + Dr Finn 37777 W. to Hospital. 1 horse destroyed. No 66416 Gunner Oram to Gen Robinsons Staff.	
	13.	Nothing to report.	
	14	Gunner Duffey from Hospital. Driver Myers from Hospital.	
	15.	Three Gunners + 1 Dr joined the Battery from Havre. 1 horse joined. Dr Crosbie to Hospital.	

Army Form C. 2118.

Instructions regarding War Diaries and Intelligence Summaries are contained in F. S. Regs., Part II, and the Staff Manual respectively. Title pages will be prepared in manuscript.

WAR DIARY
or
INTELLIGENCE SUMMARY.

(Erase heading not required.)

Hour, Date, Place.	Summary of Events and Information.	Remarks and references to Appendices
August 1915 (Cont'd)		
16	Driver Gibbons J. to Hospital.	
17.	1 L.D. Horse to Corps Remount Depot.	
18.	Nothing to Report.	
19.	" " "	
20.	Gunner Bullock rejoined from Hospital. 2 L.D. Horses joined.	
21.	Gunner Oram rejoined from Gen Robinsons Staff.	
22.	Nothing to report.	
23.	" " "	
24.	Left St HILAIRE + marched to CHIPILLY where the centre section left the Battery + proceeded into action. 1 mile NNW of SUZANNE. 2 L.D. horses went to Mobile Vet Section + 1 L.D. horse to Remount Corps Section	I.C.C.
25.	Left CHIPILLY + marched to a wagon Line to the South of Suzanne + the Left Section proceeded into action the same night, with Centre Section registered on trenches.	
26.	Completed Registration of zone allotted to Battery. Gunner Luff A. 62120 joined the Battery from "O" Bty.	
27.	QMS. Sale promoted to BSM + went to Q Battery. Sgt Copley promoted to QMS. 1 Riding horse to Mr Inchbald 121st Battery RHA. Registered on 119th Battery zone south of ours.	
28.	1 Motor Cycle orderly attached + 1 Motor Cycle. 1 Mounted Orderly attached from DAC + 1 horse.	

Army Form C. 2118.

Instructions regarding War Diaries and Intelligence Summaries are contained in F. S. Regs., Part II, and the Staff Manual respectively. Title pages will be prepared in manuscript.

WAR DIARY
or
INTELLIGENCE SUMMARY.

(Erase heading not required.)

Hour, Date, Place.	Summary of Events and Information.	Remarks and references to Appendices
August 1915 (Contd)		
28.	One gun of Right Section joined Left & Centre Sections in action.	
29.	Gunner Weller to Hospital. Br Porter rejoined from Base.	
30	No 77415 Br Churchill awarded the Medal of St George 2nd Class.	
31.	Nothing to Report.	
24th-31st	Firing confined to a few ~~rounds~~ at German ~~Trenches~~ working parties – some fired in retaliation for the Germans, shelling our ~~rounds~~ lines & occasional test rounds: No H.E. fired by order. The Battery has not been shelled yet: it was lucky that no aeroplanes came over ~~[illegible]~~ us the first few days as we were very visible then.	
	In the Field. 31st August	
	[illegible signature] Maj RHA Comdg "U" Bty RHA.	

SERIAL NO 273.

Confidential

War Diary

of

"U" Battery, Royal Horse Artillery.

FROM 1st September 1915 TO 30th November 1915.

Army Form C. 2118.

WAR DIARY

or

INTELLIGENCE SUMMARY.

(Erase heading not required.)

Instructions regarding War Diaries and Intelligence Summaries are contained in F. S. Regs., Part II, and the Staff Manual respectively. Title pages will be prepared in manuscript.

Hour, Date, Place.	Summary of Events and Information.	Remarks and references to Appendices
Suzanne 1st ~~October~~ September 1915	Gun position has now been completely concealed by the French camouflage system of painted screens. It is most satisfactory & the guns are practically invisible at a distance of a few hundred yards. Battery not located or fired at by enemy.	
2nd	Found & destroyed an observation station in German 2nd line.	
3rd	1 L.D. horse to Mo. Vety. Section.	
4th	Gunner Hughes from hospital.	
5th	Gunner Weller from hospital.	
6th	Nothing to report.	
7	Lt Dale, E.E.G. to 1st I. R.H.A. Bde. H.Q. as Adjutant, with Gr McWilliams, Dr Sharp & 2 chargers.	
8th	Gunner Adams wounded by shrapnel.	
9th	6 L.D. horses joined.	
10th	~~G~~ Nothing to report.	
11th	Nothing to report.	
12th	Battery tailor, Cpl Adams, attached. Lieut. Campbell, Gr Luff, Dr Braybrook & 2 chargers joined. Registered wire in front of German trenches on Peronne – Maricourt road.	

Instructions regarding War Diaries and Intelligence Summaries are contained in F. S. Regs., Part II, and the Staff Manual respectively. Title pages will be prepared in manuscript.

WAR DIARY

or

INTELLIGENCE SUMMARY.

(Erase heading not required.)

Army Form C. 2118.

Hour, Date, Place.		Summary of Events and Information.	Remarks and references to Appendices
Suzanne ~~October~~ September 1915	12th		
	13th	1 Officers charger & 1 light draught horse to M. V. S. 2 L. D. horses to East Surrey Regt.	
		Centre Section guns, came out of action, relieved by 2 of A98. 22nd Div. R.F.A.	
		Things very quiet all the time we were in action & nothing of interest to report. We fired H.E. for the first time & it was very satisfactory. No shell were fired by the enemy anywhere near the battery.	
	14th	"A", "E", & "F" guns out of action, relieved by 2 guns of A98. 22nd Div. R.F.A. Lt. H.W. Huggins & Gr. Weller, (servant) & 3 telephonists remain at gun position till 17 inst.	
		Battery moved at night to Frechencourt.	
	15	Battery rested till 6.30 p.m. & moved to St. Hilaire.	
	16	Lt. Campbell, with servants & chargers re-joined 1st I. RHA Bde. H.Q.	
	17	Lt. J.H. Boothby & servant (Gr. Richards) join.	
	18	2 L.D. horses transferred to H.Q. 1st Indian R.H.A. Brigade.	
	19	Nothing to report.	
	20	Gun. Watson to Havre for discharge on termination of 17 years service.	
	21st	1st I. Cavy. Division inspected by Lord Kitchener.	

Army Form C. 2118.

Instructions regarding War Diaries and Intelligence Summaries are contained in F. S. Regs., Part II, and the Staff Manual respectively. Title pages will be prepared in manuscript.

WAR DIARY

or

INTELLIGENCE SUMMARY.

(Erase heading not required.)

Hour, Date, Place.	Summary of Events and Information.	Remarks and references to Appendices
~~October~~ September 1915. 22nd	Battery moved to Heuzecourt. 1 L.D. horse to M.V.S. Dr Solomon to hospital.	
23rd	1 Officer's charger joined from 119th Battery R.F.A. for Lt. Boothby.	
24th	Gr McWilliams re-joined from 1st I. RHA Brigade.	
25th	Dr Harrigan died. (ptomaine poison) & was buried in Commune Cemetery.	
	Dr. Davies to hospital. Br. Carrington struck off as absentee. 3 L.D. horses to M.V.S	
26th	2 G.S Wagons tempory attached to Divisional ration train.	
27th	Nothing to report.	
28th	Nothing to report.	
29th	4 L.D. horses joined.	
30th	Dr Brown, A. to hospital. 1 Dvr. Shere Khan joined from A Batty	
	R. Lascelles Major R.H.A.	
	Commanding U Battery, R.H.A.	

1915

Army Form C. 2118.

Instructions regarding War Diaries and Intelligence Summaries are contained in F. S. Regs., Part II, and the Staff Manual respectively. Title pages will be prepared in manuscript.

WAR DIARY

or

INTELLIGENCE SUMMARY.

(*Erase heading not required.*)

Hour, Date, Place.		Summary of Events and Information.	Remarks and references to Appendices
Field. October.	1st.	2/Lieut. J. H. Braithwaite, R.F.A. (S.R.) attached to the Battery	
	2nd.	1 light draught horse to M.V.S. (No 29)	
	3rd.	Nothing to report	
	4th.	do.	
	5th.	do.	
	6th.	do.	
	7th.	Gr. Jones, T. E. to hospital	
	8th.	" Rose, L. do. . Cpl. Tyson transferred to 1st I. RHA Bde. H.Q.	
	9th.	Dr. Parker, A. do. . 5 Remounts joined.	
	10th.	Gr. Jones, T. E. from hospital.	
	11th.	" Dyer, F. to do . a/Brs. Webb + Willcox mustered Gunners a/Bdrs.	
	12th.	Gr. Garnham away to Havre for discharge. (T. Ex)	
	13th.	Battery marched to billets at AUTHEUX. 2Lt. Braithwaite's horse attached.	
	14th.	Drs. Hare, ~~Hayes~~ x + Rose joined from Base. x Keyse	
	15th.	4 Remounts joined 29.9.15 returned to Remount Depot.	
	16th.	1 l.d. horse joined from Remount Depot.	

1915

Army Form C. 2118.

Instructions regarding War Diaries and Intelligence Summaries are contained in F. S. Regs., Part II, and the Staff Manual respectively. Title pages will be prepared in manuscript.

WAR DIARY

or

INTELLIGENCE SUMMARY.

(Erase heading not required.)

Hour, Date, Place.		Summary of Events and Information.	Remarks and references to Appendices
Field October	17th.	Capt. Rolleston's charger to M.V.S.	
	18th.	Nothing to report.	
	19th.	Gr. Duffy & Elgin to hospital. I Dvr. Khuda Bux to hospl.	
	20th.	Two L.D. horses to M.V.S. Drs. Darley, O'Brien, Tanner, & Telfer joined.	
	21st.	Three L.D. horses to M.V.S.	
	22nd.	Battery marched to billets at FOURDRINOY.	
	23rd.	Captain Rolleston posted to battery in England.	
	24th.	Nothing to report.	
	25th.	Nothing to report.	
	26th.	Nothing to report.	
	27th.	Seven remounts joined from Remount Depôt.	
	28th.	Two L.D. horses to M.V.S.	
	29th.	Gr. Fleming, A. to hospital.	
	30th.	Nothing to report.	
	31st.	Do.	

Field
31st. October 1915.

M. Lascelles
Major R.H.A.
Commandg. U Battery R.H.A.

Army Form C. 2118.

Instructions regarding War Diaries and Intelligence Summaries are contained in F. S. Regs., Part II, and the Staff Manual respectively. Title pages will be prepared in manuscript.

WAR DIARY

or

INTELLIGENCE SUMMARY.

(Erase heading not required.)

Hour, Date, Place.	Summary of Events and Information.	Remarks and references to Appendices
Fourdrinoy. Nov 1st 1915.	Sadd. Friend, Gr. Aston, Capstick, & Harvey joined. Lieut. C. F. Campbell, 2 batmen[x], & two horses attached.	[x] Gr. Luff & Dr. Braybrook.
2nd	Driver Tanner to hospital.	
3rd & 4th.	Nothing to report.	
5th.	Gunner Fleming re-joins from Hospital.	
6th & 7th.	Nothing to report.	
8th.	Major R. H. Lascelles presented with medal, Chevalier, Legion d'Honneur.	by G.O.C. 1st Indian Cavalry Division
	Cpl. S. Nokes presented with Croix de Guerre.	at Airaines.
9th.	Sergt R. Holmes to New Army, England	on promotion.
10th.	" C Wallis to hospital.	
11th.	2/Lieut Dr. G. J. Kemm attached to the battery.	
12th & 13th.	Nothing to report.	
14th.	2/Lieut H. G. Morrison & 2 batmen to ~~New Army~~ R.F.A.[x] Bdr. Liley to 139 Bde. R.F.A.	[x] H.Q. 28th Brigade. 5th Division
	Indian Dr. Prenda Khan transferred from Q Battery RHA.	
15th & 16th.	Nothing to report.	
17th.	(2) Two light draught horses to the Mobile Veterinary Section.	

Army Form C. 2118.

WAR DIARY

or

INTELLIGENCE SUMMARY.

(*Erase heading not required.*)

Instructions regarding War Diaries and Intelligence Summaries are contained in F. S. Regs., Part II, and the Staff Manual respectively. Title pages will be prepared in manuscript.

Hour, Date, Place.	Summary of Events and Information.	Remarks and references to Appendices
Fourdrinoy 18th Novemb.r 1915	The battery marched to billets at BETTENCOURT-sur-SOMME.	
20th "	The battery marched to billets at METIGNY & LALEU.x	x centre section.
22nd "	Two men joined from 1st. I.C.D. Ammn. Column.	Gun.r Ball & Dr. Speight.
24th "	I. Driver Mohamed Panah joined from Genl. Ind.n Base Depôt. Marseilles	
25th "	Gunners Richards & Simms to hospital	
27th "	Five light draught horses to the Remount Depot.	
28th "	Gnrs. Putnam & Thacker, Drivers Quigley & Rosen, joined.	
30th "	Gnrs. Doyle & Miller to hospital. One light draught horse destroyed.	
	[signature] Major R.H.A. Commanding U Battery R.H.A.	

SERIAL NO 273.

Confidential

War Diary

of

"U" Battery, Royal Horse Artillery.

FROM 1st December 1915 TO 31st December 1915.

"W" Battery R.H.A.

WAR DIARY

or

INTELLIGENCE SUMMARY.

(*Erase heading not required.*)

Army Form C. 2118.

Instructions regarding War Diaries and Intelligence Summaries are contained in F. S. Regs., Part II, and the Staff Manual respectively. Title pages will be prepared in manuscript.

Hour, Date, Place. 1915.	Summary of Events and Information.	Remarks and references to Appendices
Metigny-l'abbé December 1st.	Nothing to report.	
5th.	Nine light draught horses joined from Remount Depôt.	
7th.	Gr. Lacey E. Gr. Price. Dr. Smith, H. & Dr. Small, joined from Ammn. Col.	
9th.	Dr. M. Rosen sent to Havre for discharge, under age.	
10th.	Battery marched to FRECHENCOURT. Bdr. Cecil reduced to "Gunner". Dr. Tucker to hospl.	
	Drs. Milne - Philp, 4 horses & 1 G.S. wagon, A.S.C. attached, for horse rugs.	
15th.	Bdr. C. F. Carrington re-joined, under escort.	
16th.	Bdr. C. F. Carrington to hospital.[x] Two light draught horses to M.V.S.	x mental case.
18th.	Battery marched to LAVIEVILLE.	
19th.	Seven men attached from 1st. I.C.D. Ammn. Column.	Bdr. Abell, Gr. Elliott, " Jones, " Semple, " Salmon, " Cattel, " Wise.
23rd.	Cpl. A. Wright joined from No. 2 Genl. Base.	
31st.	Two light draught horses transferred to the Royal Engineers.	

C.R.
780
8/2/16

Army Form C. 2118.

Instructions regarding War Diaries and Intelligence Summaries are contained in F. S. Regs., Part II, and the Staff Manual respectively. Title pages will be prepared in manuscript.

WAR DIARY
or
INTELLIGENCE SUMMARY.

(Erase heading not required.)

Hour, Date, Place.	Summary of Events and Information.	Remarks and references to Appendices
Lavièville - 18th to 31st Dec. 1915	The battery has been 'Sniping & Enfilading' from forward positions. Guns have been sent up singly, or two at a time when it has been wished to enfilade trenches from both flanks simultaneously. Positions have been on front of 18th & 51st Divisions. Generally 200 - 250 rounds ammn has been allowed a week, & 4 or 5 Guns have gone up weekly. They go up by night, shoot next day & come away that night. The ground on the right of both Divns ~~lands also~~ is well adapted to these operations, on the left not so well.	
Field 1st Jany 1916.	J H Boothby Lt for Major RHA Commanding U Battery RHA	

SERIAL NO 273.

Confidential

War Diary

of

"U" Battery, Royal Horse Artillery

FROM 1st January 1918 TO 31st January 1918

Instructions regarding War Diaries and Intelligence Summaries are contained in F. S. Regs., Part II. and the Staff Manual respectively. Title Pages will be prepared in manuscript.

1916 III

WAR DIARY
or
INTELLIGENCE SUMMARY
(Erase heading not required.)

"U" Battery R. H. A.

Army Form C. 2118

(1)

Place	Date	Hour	Summary of Events and Information	Remarks and references to Appendices
LAVIEVILLE	1st January		Two horses away. 1 to Mobile Vety. Section & 1 to R. Engineers.	
	7th.	"	Four guns took up position in the grounds of Chateau d'Aussy on outskirts of ALBERT to defend a section of the trench line. "A" Battery, 83rd. Brigade R.F.A. was relieved & went to rest.	
	11th.	"	Gunners Wise & Putnam to hospital. Sergt. Wallis, Gunners Elgin & Richards rejoined from Base.	
	13th.	"	Gunner Honeybun to hospital.	
	14th.		Naick Burhan Ali & Dvr. Speight to hospital.	
	28th.	"	Driver Bywater transferred from "B" Battery. 84th. Bde. R.F.A.	
	31st.	"	The four guns left the position at ALBERT, where they were relieved by "A" Batty. 83rd. Bde. R.F.A.	
			During the whole month the battery was engaged on sniping & enfilading work; till the 7th. with 6 guns & from then to the 31st. with 2 guns & the remaining 4 in position as above.	
			12 or 15 different positions were occupied with single guns or sections for periods varying from 1 to 5 days. The guns used enfilade fire from positions near the trenches, both on their own & in co-operation with others in several small shows, at times they were pushed up to bring fire on roads & other points where traffic was visible which could not be reached by guns in position, & had several very successful shoots at parties & transport of the enemy. The positions used were on the front of the 5th.	CR 848 D/28/2/16

1875 Wt. W593/826 1,000,000 4/15 J.B.C. & A. A.D.S.S./Forms/C. 2118.

Instructions regarding War Diaries and Intelligence Summaries are contained in F. S. Regs., Part II. and the Staff Manual respectively. Title Pages will be prepared in manuscript.

1916

WAR DIARY
or
INTELLIGENCE SUMMARY
(Erase heading not required.)

III

Army Form. C. 2118 (2)

M Battery. R.H.A.

Place	Date	Hour	Summary of Events and Information	Remarks and references to Appendices
LAVIEVILLE	31st. January		-of the 5th, 18th. & 32nd. Divisions, roughly from the Somme to Martinsart.	
			No high explosive was allowed to be used owing to bad fuzes.	
			The sniping guns were on no occasion located by the enemy and the battery had no casualties.	
			Field [illegible] Major R.H.A.	
			31st. January 1916. Commanding M Battery R.H.A.	

1875 Wt. W593/826 1,000,000 4/15 J.B.C. & A. A.D.S.S./Forms/C. 2118.

SERIAL NO 273.

Confidential

War Diary

of

"U" Battery, Royal Horse Artillery

FROM 1st February 1916 TO 29th February 1916

Instructions regarding War Diaries and Intelligence Summaries are contained in F. S. Regs., Part II. and the Staff Manual respectively. Title Pages will be prepared in manuscript.

WAR DIARY
or
INTELLIGENCE SUMMARY
(Erase heading not required.)

Army Form C. 2118

1916 "U" Battery. R.H.A.

Place	Date	Hour	Summary of Events and Information	Remarks and references to Appendices
Lavieville	3rd February		Battery left Lavieville and marched to Querrieu. Six men I C D Ammunition Column returned to unit.	
	4th	--	Battery marched to Condé Folie. One horse destroyed.	
	5th	--	Battery marched to Ochancourt.	
Ochancourt	7th	--	Dr. Philip & Milne 4 horses & G.S. wagon to A.S.C.	
	8th	--	G. Elgin to Hospital 3/2/16. One Light Draught horse to Mobile Vet: Section 18th Div	
	15th	--	~~4~~ horses joined from Remount Dept.	
	16th	--	~~Two remounts returned to Remount Dept.~~	
	21st	--	One L D horse to Mobile Vet. Section	
	27th	--	Three remounts joined	
	28th	--	G. Symes to hospital	
	29th	--	D. Mitchell to hospital.	

Field
29. 2. 16

W Lascelles.
Major R.H.A.
Commanding "U" Battery RHA

1875 Wt. W593/826 1,000,000 4/15 J.B.C. & A. A.D.S.S./Forms/C. 2118.

SERIAL NO 273.

Confidential

War Diary

of

"U" Battery, Royal Horse Artillery

FROM 1st March 1916 TO 31st March 1916.

Instructions regarding War Diaries and Intelligence Summaries are contained in F. S. Regs., Part II. and the Staff Manual respectively. Title Pages will be prepared in manuscript.

III

WAR DIARY
or
INTELLIGENCE SUMMARY
(Erase heading not required.)

"U" Battery R.H.A.
March 1916.

Army Form C. 2118

Place	Date	Hour	Summary of Events and Information	Remarks and references to Appendices
Ochancourt	2 3/16		S.S. Dr. A. Lacey to hospital. Q.M.S. Copley promoted 2/Lieut. & proceeds to Havre. Grs. Clarke, C.F. Brown, F.J. Croxon, A. Hanrahan, H. & Williams, E. transfer to Ammn. in exchange for Grs. Broder, Boss, FitzGerald, Godfrey, & Chorlton	
	4th.		Cpl. Tyson joined from 1st Ind. R.H.A. Bde. Headquarters. One light draught joined from Remount Depot.	
	7th.		One riding horse transferred to Lucknow Cav. Bde. Staff.	
	8th.		Sergt. Maddox joined from Ammn. Col. on probation for Q.M.S.	
	15th.		Ind. Driv. Abdulla Khan to Marseilles for India.	
	18th.		Dr. Wager to hospital. 19th. Cpl. Tyson to hospital. 20th. Two l.d. horses to M.V.S.	
	21st.		Tr. Ashley joined from Ammn. Col. One light draught horse joined. One riding horse to "A" Batty. R.H.A.	
	22nd.		Cpl. Wright transferred to Ammn. Park. Interpreter, Mons. Deleuze leaves the battery.	
	26th.		Battery marched to TOLLENT. Men under cover, horses in the open.	
	27th.		Bomb. Eldrington to hospital. 28th. Gunner Pell to hospital	
	30th.		One l.d. horse to M.V.S. Capt. Huggins, Sergt. Wallis, Cpl. Crowhurst attached to 55th Div.	also Gr. Weller (servant)
	31st.		One l.d. horse to M.V.S.	
			Field. 31-3-16. [signature] Major R.H.A. Commanding "U" Battery R.H.A.	

SERIAL NO 273.

Confidential

War Diary

of

"U" Battery, Royal Horse Artillery

FROM 1st April 1916 TO 30th April 1916.

18/5

Instructions regarding War Diaries and Intelligence Summaries are contained in F. S. Regs., Part II. and the Staff Manual respectively. Title Pages will be prepared in manuscript.

April 1916.

WAR DIARY or INTELLIGENCE SUMMARY

(Erase heading not required.)

U Battery. R.H.A. III.

Army Form C. 2118

Place	Date April	Hour	Summary of Events and Information	Remarks and references to Appendices
TOLLENT 1916.	1st		Interpreter Vicomte E. d'Herneau joined in relief of Mons. Deleuze.	
	2nd		One horse transferred from 'A' Battery R.H.A.	(Desmond)
	5th		Bdr. Eldrington re-joined from Hospital. Dvr. McP. O'Brien transferred to 'A' Batty. R.H.A.	
	6th		Cpl. Tyson re-joined from Hospital. 9th Gunr. T. Berry to hospital.	
	9th		Battery marches to AGENVILLERS for Brigade & Divisional training	
	10th	13th	Ind. Dvr. Nur Khan, No. 9159, joins. Saddler A. J. Friend transferred to Ammn. Column.	
	14th		Four Drivers, A.E. Taylor, J.E. Hicks, A. Donaldson, & R. Ford, join from Ammn. Column.	
	17th		79982 Cpl. E. Thornley joins battery. One horse transferred to 'A' Battery. R.H.A.	
	18th		Arm. S. Sjt. Willis, W.E. joins to relieve Arm. S. Sjt. Barnes, S. who leaves on 26th inst.	
	19th		Gunner J.R. Thacker to hospital. 25th No. 72068 Gr. E. Peckham joins from 49th Batty. R.F.A.	{younger brother to 50480 G. Peckham
	28th		Two light draught horses (194 & 197) to M.V.S.	
	30th		13 Pdr. Q.F. guns & wagons exchanged for 18 Pdr. Q.F.	

Field. 30th April 1916.

J.H. Boothby Lt for Major R.H.A.
Commanding U Batty. R.H.A.

SERIAL NO 273.

Confidential

War Diary

of

"U" Battery, Royal Horse Artillery.

FROM 1st May 1916 TO 31st May 1916.

Instructions regarding War Diaries and Intelligence Summaries are contained in F. S. Regs., Part II. and the Staff Manual respectively. Title Pages will be prepared in manuscript.

Army Form C. 2118

WAR DIARY *or* INTELLIGENCE SUMMARY

(Erase heading not required.)

May 1916 "U" Battery R. H. A.

Place	Date	Hour	Summary of Events and Information	Remarks and references to Appendices
AGENVILLERS	May.	1st	Ind. Dvr. Azimullah Khan to hospital. Driver Earnshaw to hospital. 3rd Driver M. P. O'Brien transferred to "A" Batty. R.H.A.	
	-"-	7th.	Battery marches to TOLLENT. 1 horse transferred to 29th Lancers 1 Remount joined. No. 79587 Gr. O.W.L. Cox joined.	
	-"-	10th.	Battery marches to REBREUVE. Charger "Desmond" to Capt. A. G. Rolleston.	
	-"-	14th.	No. 126692 Gunr. J. Andrews joins. 17th. B.S.M. Brooks G. to hospital. Dr. Telfer transfd. to 169 Bde. R.F.A.	
	-"-	18th.	Battery marches to MINGOVAL. 19th. Centre Section took over 2 guns in action ~~near~~ at F12. A94.	
	-"-	21st.	Right Section joined Left & battery took over 4 guns in middle of heavy hostile bombardment of our positions on VIMY RIDGE. The front & support line of "Q" Sector were captured on a front of about 1500 yds. German Infy. attacking at about 7-45 p.m. 23rd. 3 Remounts joined. 24th. Registered in morning. 25th. -ditto-	
	-"-	26th.	Moved Right & Left sections out of action to a farm at F9. B28. which it was intended to use as a H.Q. whilst making a 4 gun position at F11. A37. Gunr. A. J. King to hospital. Ind. Driver Lal Din joined.	
	-"-	27th.	One horse transferred to "D" Batty. 111th Bde. 29th. Ind. Dr. Nur Khan joined. Gr. A. Mayes. Dr. L. Evans joined.	
	-"-	30th.	Took over responsibility in new position at 11.0. p.m. all guns being then in. Registration carried out just after dawn this morning.	
	-"-	31st.	Gr. Newbery, Gr. Raynor, Dr. Hunt, & Dr. Warnaby joined.	

[signature] Major RHA
Commanding "U" Batty. RHA.

SERIAL NO 273.

Confidential

War Diary

of

"U" Battery, Royal Horse Artillery

FROM 1st June 1916 TO 30th June 1916

Instructions regarding War Diaries and Intelligence Summaries are contained in F. S. Regs., Part II. and the Staff Manual respectively. Title Pages will be prepared in manuscript.

U Battery R.H.A. III

WAR DIARY or INTELLIGENCE SUMMARY

(Erase heading not required.)

June 1916 (1)

Army Form C. 2118

Place	Date	Hour	Summary of Events and Information	Remarks and references to Appendices
F11. A37 near Mt St ELOY	1/6/16		Wagon lines moved to ACQ.	
	3/6/16		No. 103 Dr. Buckley to Havre for discharge.	
	4/6/16		New Obs^n Post completed.	
	5th & 6th →		Registering.	
	7th		Alternative Obs^n Post reconnoitred & work commenced.	
	9/6/16		2 light draught horses transferr^d to A Batty 256 Bde.	
	14/6/16		One light draught horse transf^d to M.V.S.	
	16/6/16		C/9494 Rifleman A Porter transf^d to U Battery RHA	

1875 Wt. W593/826 1,000,000 4/15 J.B.C. & A. A.D.S.S./Forms/C. 2118.

Instructions regarding War Diaries and Intelligence Summaries are contained in F. S. Regs., Part II. and the Staff Manual respectively. Title Pages will be prepared in manuscript.

"U" Battery R.H.A. 1/III

WAR DIARY
or
INTELLIGENCE SUMMARY
(Erase heading not required.)

June 1916. (2)

Army Form C. 2118

Place	Date	Hour	Summary of Events and Information	Remarks and references to Appendices
F 11. A 37 near M^t. S^t. ELOY.	21/6		Assist. Surg^n. E. E. Copcutt ceases to do duty with the battery.	
	25/6/16		Dvr. Keyse sent to Base. (under-age). Ptz Turner, U.A. transf^d from Cyclists. 10717 Pte. H.P. Nokes transf^d from 2nd Wilts. One l.d. horse to M.V.S.	
	28th.		Battery position has not been found by enemy & never had a shell near it.	
	29th.		Moved out of action to ACQ. Dr. Smith W. to Hospital	
	29th.		Battery marched to REBREUVE. Gnr Howlett, to Hospital.	
	30th.		Battery marched to DOULLENS.	

H. Lascelles Major R.H.A.
Commanding U Battery R.H.A.

1875 Wt. W593/826 1,000,000 4/15 J.B.C. & A. A.D.S.S./Forms/C. 2118.

SERIAL NO 273.

Confidential

War Diary

of

"U" Battery, Royal Horse Artillery

FROM 1st July 1916 TO 31st July 1916.

Instructions regarding War Diaries and Intelligence Summaries are contained in F. S. Regs., Part II. and the Staff Manual respectively. Title Pages will be prepared in manuscript.

July 1916

WAR DIARY
or.
INTELLIGENCE SUMMARY
(Erase heading not required.)

U Battery R.H.A. III

Army Form C. 2118

Place	Date	Hour	Summary of Events and Information	Remarks and references to Appendices
DOULLENS.	1st.		Dr. W. Simms to hospital.	
	2nd.		Battery marched to BEAUVOIR-RIVIERE.	
	4th.		Drivers Allen, R. & Darley, L.S. to hospital. Gunr. Howlett, W. re-joined.	
	5th.		Gunner Aston & Driver Warnaby to hospital.	
	8th.		Driver Hunt to hospital.	
	9th.		Six remounts joined.	
	14th.		Indian Driver Shanker joined. 15th. Driver J. Crosbie joined.	
	16th.		Seven remounts join. 7 horses transferred to Cavalry Regts. 1 horse to Q Battery R.H.A.	
	18th.		Battery marched to HEILLY & attached to 28th Brigade R.F.A. 5th Division. XV Corps.	
	19th.		Battery marched to BECORDEL. Gunr. Godfrey to hospital.	
	20th.		The battery went into a position S. of MONTAUBAN by day. Major's Friend party & Battery Staff used complete & mounted wirelaying was employed. A good observation station was found in a sap from the old 2nd line close to LONGUEVAL.	
	21st.		The Right Section moved to a forward position about 1000x S.W. of LONGUEVAL. Whilst here the section lost 1 Killed & 3 wounded. (Gr. Lacy. Gr. Unwin. Grs. Till & Capstick)	
	22nd.		2/Lieut. J. L. Braithwaite Killed. Gunr. Chorlton wounded. Horse No. 183 to M.V.S. Gr. Davis A. & Driver Webb, E. to hospital.	
	23rd.		Lieut. J. H. Boothby Killed. Gr. Unwin & Gr. Till wounded. Gr. Cattell & Dr. Tonge join.	
	24th.		Gr. E. Lacy Killed. Gunr. E. Capstick wounded. The right Section came back to the battery position	

1875 Wt. W593/826 1,000,000 4/15 J.B.C. & A. A.D.S.S./Forms/C. 2118.

(continued)

Instructions regarding War Diaries and Intelligence Summaries are contained in F. S. Regs., Part II. and the Staff Manual respectively. Title Pages will be prepared in manuscript.

July 1916.

WAR DIARY
or
INTELLIGENCE SUMMARY
(Erase heading not required.)

U Battery R.H.A.

III.

Army Form C. 2118

Place	Date	Hour	Summary of Events and Information	Remarks and references to Appendices
	25th		The battery was heavily shelled with 8", 5·9, 4·2, & 77 mm. Gr. Howlett Killed, Lieut C. F. Campbell, Sergt. Silvester, a/Cpl. Greenaway, Bdr. Bywater, Gunners Cecil, Noakes, Williams, & Willis wounded. One direct hit removed "F" Sub section wagon & "E" Sub sections wagon caught fire but was extinguished. The battery took part in the bombardment of DELVILLE WOOD before its capture by the 5th Division. In all 3600 rounds were fired from 4 guns in the 24 hours. Dr. Pearson to hospital.	
	26th		Fitter & Sgt. Roberts to hospital. 2/Lieut. W.K. Holmes attached for duty. Gr. H Whitehead attached for duty. Gnr. Fox, Gnr. Wade, Dr. Harrison, Gr. Foster join.	
	27th		One gun under 2/Lt. W.K. Holmes assisted an attack by the 51st. Divn. by bombarding the sunken road running S.E. from the E. corner of High Wood. The gun was in an advanced position 300x S. of S.W. end of LONGUEVAL, & the observing was carried out from a point which was heavily barraged by the enemy. 93 rounds of H.E. were fired in 30 minutes. Gunners Ilsley, Cartwright, Roberts, A.W. Collins, Page, Elliott, & Oram joined. a/Bdr. Oram & Driver Hicks wounded.	
	27th		Gnrs. Perkins & Roberts, F.W. & Dr. O. King joined. Gnr. Skinner to hospital. One horse Killed.	
	29th		The battery had its first cessation of fire to-day having fired for 108 hours continuously. After 3 hours fire was resumed. 2/Lieut. St. J. G. Kemm & 2/Lieut. W.K. Holmes wounded, but remain at duty.	
	30th		Dr. O. King wounded. a/Br. Chapman wounded, but remains at duty. Gr. Carrington to hospital. One horse Killed. Gr. A. Davis rejoined from hospital.	
	31st		a/Bdr. Edwards to hospital.	

W. Higgins. Capt. RHA
Commanding U Battery RHA.

1875 Wt. W593/826 1,000,000 4/15 J.B.C. & A. A.D.S.S./Forms/C. 2118.

Instructions regarding War Diaries and Intelligence Summaries are contained in F. S. Regs., Part II. and the Staff Manual respectively. Title Pages will be prepared in manuscript.

WAR DIARY
or
INTELLIGENCE SUMMARY

(Erase heading not required.)

[illegible] 1916 — [illegible] Battery [illegible]

Army Form C. 2118

Place	Date	Hour	Summary of Events and Information	Remarks and references to Appendices
			[illegible] Davies wounded. 2 Horses killed by Shell fire. Gr Carrington to Hospital	
			[illegible] S [illegible] & 111086 Dr G H [illegible] joined from D.A.C.	
			[illegible] to Hospital	
			[illegible] to Hospital. Bdr Chapman wounded but remained at duty.	
			[illegible] H [illegible], Gun [illegible] & Dr Watts S to 25th Brigade R.F.A. 1st Div.	
			[illegible] rejoined from Hospital	
			[illegible] Section gun destroyed by Hostile Shell. 'C' Sub Section Gun damaged by Hostile Shell and taken to wagon line for repair. 4 Guns handed over in action to 12th Batty	
			[illegible] 'A' Batty detachments etc go to Wagon line for 2 days. Dr Ashley rejoined [illegible] Bowers joined. Following draft from D.A.C. 40461 Gr Chatfield	
			[illegible] Gr [illegible], 5136 Gr Joyce J, 59514 Gr Dixon D, 80153 Gr [illegible] R, 35085 Gr Crouch [illegible]	
			[illegible] Dr Young [illegible], 59645 Dr Salt E, 27555 Dr Clark F, 102634 Dr Blamon [illegible], 5725 Dr Hill [illegible]	
			[illegible] following men rejoined D.A.C. Gun [illegible], Gr Roberts J, Gr Ilsley, Gr Foster, Gr Wade, [illegible], Gr [illegible] A, Dr Harrison, Dr [illegible], Dr [illegible], Dr Turner.	
			[illegible] reverted to Gunner at his own request.	
			[illegible] notification that [illegible] proceeded to England 30th [illegible]	
			[illegible] to Gun Position 10 am.	
			[illegible] [illegible], 58115 Gr Foster, 42921 Dr Day H; [illegible] Goodlove, 72002 Peters, 57342 Wood; [illegible] Salt, 57553 Dr Hodgkinson, 64958 [illegible]; [illegible] Oliver, 11084 Turner G, [illegible] [illegible] } joined from D A C	49302 Gr [illegible] joined [illegible] [illegible]. Dr Matthews from Hospital to [illegible]. Gr [illegible] to Hospital. Horse [illegible] destroyed [illegible]

1875 W. W593/826 1,000,000 4/15 J.B.C. & A. A.D.S.S./Forms/C. 2118.

Army Form C. 2118

Instructions regarding War Diaries and Intelligence Summaries are contained in F. S. Regs., Part II. and the Staff Manual respectively. Title Pages will be prepared in manuscript.

WAR DIARY
or
INTELLIGENCE SUMMARY
(Erase heading not required.)

August 1916 "U" Battery R.H.A. 919

Place	Date	Hour	Summary of Events and Information	Remarks and references to Appendices
[illegible]	11th		39692 Gunner H Bullock wounded	
	12th		60148 Churchill W transferred to 25th Brigade R.F.A.	
	13th		Gunner Bryant C to Hospital	
			Driver Gulford from Hospital	
	14th		Major E Rich joined from B/90 Battery R.F.A.	
			2/Lieut E J S Cowling joined from "A" Battery R.H.A.	
			80824 Dr Donaldson awarded 14 days Field Punishment No 1.	

Instructions regarding War Diaries and Intelligence Summaries are contained in F. S. Regs., Part II. and the Staff Manual respectively. Title Pages will be prepared in manuscript.

WAR DIARY
or
INTELLIGENCE SUMMARY
(Erase heading not required.)

August 1916 — "C" Battery 8th Bde — [illegible]

Army Form C. 2118

Place	Date	Hour	Summary of Events and Information	Remarks and references to Appendices
[illegible]	[illegible]	9am	Battery was relieved by 123 Battery and went to Wagon line for 3 days rest	
		1pm	B.C. [illegible] for by OC 28th Brigade R.F.A. and ordered to bring battery into action again at 6 pm.	
			B.C. [illegible] Capt Huggins reconnoitred for a position for a forward section and selected one just W of TRONES WOOD	

Army Form C. 2118

Instructions regarding War Diaries and Intelligence Summaries are contained in F. S. Regs., Part II. and the Staff Manual respectively. Title Pages will be prepared in manuscript.

WAR DIARY
or
INTELLIGENCE SUMMARY
(Erase heading not required.)

August 1916 — "C" Battery R.H.A. — 921

Place	Date	Hour	Summary of Events and Information	Remarks and references to Appendices
	[illegible]	[illegible]	[illegible] sent to TRONES WOOD & registered	
			[illegible] Blake R and [illegible] wounded. Both remained at duty	
			[illegible] Rowley wounded	

1875 Wt. W593/826 1,000,000 4/15 J.B.C. & A. A.D.S.S./Forms/C. 2118.

Instructions regarding War Diaries and Intelligence Summaries are contained in F. S. Regs., Part II. and the Staff Manual respectively. Title Pages will be prepared in manuscript.

Army Form C. 2118

WAR DIARY
or
INTELLIGENCE SUMMARY
(Erase heading not required.)

August 1916   U Battery R.H.A.   922

Place	Date	Hour	Summary of Events and Information	Remarks and references to Appendices
	[illegible]	[illegible]am	[illegible] Capt Huggins did a reconnaissance of the NE corner of DELVILLE WOOD with a view to [illegible] for the coming action but were shelled out of it by British Guns which were falling short, which also cut their wire.	
		[illegible]	[illegible] hot Guns went to forward position 500 yards W of TRONES and were registered on their target.	
			Unfortunately a premature from one of "U" Bty Guns killed a man of the [illegible] Bty who were in action immediately in front.	
			[illegible] the afternoon the personnel of 40th Battery took refuge in U Bty position [illegible] their own being heavily shelled.	

1875 Wt. W593/826 1,000,000 4/15 J.B.C. & A. A.D.S.S./Forms/C. 2118.

Diaries and Intelligence
... S. Regs., Part II.
... Title Pages

Army Form C. 2118

WAR DIARY
or
INTELLIGENCE SUMMARY
(Erase heading not required.)

August 1916 — "W" Battery R.F.A. — 923

Hour	Summary of Events and Information	Remarks and references to Appendices
	attack on whole front. Battery covered NE ~~end~~ of DELVILLE WOOD, where the infantry	
	... their objectives, which were BEER & BITTER TRENCHES. The	
	...f Brigadier sent a wire later saying "The artillery barrage was	
	...cent and perfect in its regularity. The Infantry were enabled to	
	...t right up under it with the utmost confidence"	
	...orward section under Lieut Bartling did excellent work firing at a	
	... of 1900 yards.	
...0	...d Section returned to Battery position without a casualty. This is	
	...ue to the use of camouflage screens over the guns.	
	...aylor and Darnaby to Hosp.	
	... Oakley and 2 Gunners joined from B/90 Battery R.F.A.	

1875 Wt. W593/826 1,000,000 4/15 J.B.C. & A. A.D.S.S./Forms/C. 2118.

Instructions regarding War Diaries and Intelligence Summaries are contained in F. S. Regs., Part II. and the Staff Manual respectively. Title Pages will be prepared in manuscript.

WAR DIARY or INTELLIGENCE SUMMARY

(Erase heading not required.)

August 1916 — H Battery R.H.A. [?]

Army Form C. 2118

924

Place	Date	Hour	Summary of Events and Information	Remarks and references to Appendices
Montauban	19th		Gunner [?] H Bollery [?] joined from A R.H.A.	
			Gunner Edmonds [?] joined from B/90 R.F.A.	
			Horse [?] to 25th Brigade R.F.A.	
			Bomb Ellington [?] promoted Corpl vice Churchill from 12/8/16	
			SaBdr Turner W appd Bdr from 23/8/16 vice Chapman	
			Gunners Gabbitas & Creighton appd SaBdrs.	
			Gunner Naylor wounded	

1875 Wt. W593/826 1,000,000 4/15 J.B.C. & A. A.D.S.S./Forms/C. 2118.

Army Form C. 2118

Instructions regarding War Diaries and Intelligence Summaries are contained in F. S. Regs., Part II. and the Staff Manual respectively. Title Pages will be prepared in manuscript.

WAR DIARY
or
INTELLIGENCE SUMMARY

(Erase heading not required.)

Place	Date	Hour	Summary of Events and Information	Remarks and references to Appendices

1875 Wt. W593/826 1,000,000 4/15 J.B.C. & A. A.D.S.S./Forms/C. 2118.

Instructions regarding War Diaries and Intelligence Summaries are contained in F. S. Regs., Part II. and the Staff Manual respectively. Title Pages will be prepared in manuscript.

WAR DIARY

or

INTELLIGENCE SUMMARY

(Erase heading not required.)

August 1916 — [illegible] Battery R.H.A.

Army Form C. 2118

a26

Place	Date	Hour	Summary of Events and Information	Remarks and references to Appendices
	[illegible]		[illegible] attacked along the whole front but did no good	
			[illegible] Gunner [illegible] wounded.	
			[illegible] Money or effect Clarke "Williams" charger to [illegible] Section	

1875 Wt. W593/826 1,000,000 4/15 J.B.C. & A. A.D.S.S./Forms/C. 2118.

Instructions regarding War Diaries and Intelligence Summaries are contained in F. S. Regs., Part II. and the Staff Manual respectively. Title Pages will be prepared in manuscript.

August 1916

WAR DIARY
or
INTELLIGENCE SUMMARY
(Erase heading not required.)

U Battery R.H.A.

Army Form C. 2118

927

Place	Date	Hour	Summary of Events and Information	Remarks and references to Appendices
			[illegible] brought out of action and placed in position [illegible]	
			[illegible] These guns taken over by detachments of 123 Battery [illegible]	
			remaining two guns in battery position	
			[illegible] to hospital	
			[illegible] wounded	
			[illegible] killed	

1875 Wt. W593/826 1,000,000 4/15 J.B.C. & A. A.D.S.S./Forms/C. 2118.

Instructions regarding War Diaries and Intelligence Summaries are contained in F. S. Regs., Part II. and the Staff Manual respectively. Title Pages will be prepared in manuscript.

Army Form C. 2118

WAR DIARY
or
INTELLIGENCE SUMMARY
(Erase heading not required.)

August 1916. 91st Battery R.F.A. 926

Place	Date	Hour	Summary of Events and Information	Remarks and references to Appendices
Montauban	23rd		Corpl Broadhurst A appointed acting Sergt from 25/8/16 vice Silvester	
			Bomr Webb G " " Corpl " " vice Broadhurst	
			A/Bdr Chapman C " " Bomb^r " 23/8/16 [illegible]	
			A/Bdr Buskin S " " " 25/8/16 " Bywater	
			[illegible] R Gore to Hospital	

1875 Wt. W593/826 1,000,000 4/15 J.B.C. & A. A.D.S.S./Forms/C. 2118.

Instructions regarding War Diaries and Intelligence Summaries are contained in F. S. Regs., Part II. and the Staff Manual respectively. Title Pages will be prepared in manuscript.

August 1916

WAR DIARY
or
INTELLIGENCE SUMMARY
(Erase heading not required.)

[illegible] Battery R.F.A.

Army Form C. 2118

929

Place	Date	Hour	Summary of Events and Information	Remarks and references to Appendices
[illegible]	24th		Lieut. J.J.S. Gosling wounded by premature of 65th Battery, (Remained at duty)	
			Battery took part in the bombardment with the object of driving the enemy from DELVILLE WOOD which was accomplished	
			One gun received from Ordnance Shops	

1875 Wt. W593/826 1,000,000 4/15 J.B.C. & A. A.D.S.S./Forms/C. 2118.

WAR DIARY
or
INTELLIGENCE SUMMARY
(Erase heading not required.)

Army Form C. 2118

930

Instructions regarding War Diaries and Intelligence Summaries are contained in F. S. Regs., Part II. and the Staff Manual respectively. Title Pages will be prepared in manuscript.

August 1916. [illegible]

Place	Date	Hour	Summary of Events and Information	Remarks and references to Appendices
Montauban	25th		New position 100x N of BERNAFAY Wood selected & work commenced on it – A fearful journey with wagons of material owing to crump holes & many wagons were broken –	
			[illegible] Gnr [illegible] Gill awarded Military Medal 19/8/16	
			[illegible] rejoined from Hospital	
			[illegible] evacuated to Hospital	

Army Form C. 2118

Instructions regarding War Diaries and Intelligence Summaries are contained in F. S. Regs., Part II. and the Staff Manual respectively. Title Pages will be prepared in manuscript.

WAR DIARY
or
INTELLIGENCE SUMMARY
(Erase heading not required.)

August 1916 [illegible] 931

Place	Date	Hour	Summary of Events and Information	Remarks and references to Appendices
[illegible]	26th		[illegible]	

1875 Wt. W593/826 1,000,000 4/15 J.B.C. & A. A.D.S.S./Forms/C. 2118.

Instructions regarding War Diaries and Intelligence Summaries are contained in F. S. Regs., Part II. and the Staff Manual respectively. Title Pages will be prepared in manuscript.

WAR DIARY
or
INTELLIGENCE SUMMARY
(Erase heading not required.)

Army Form C. 2118

August 1916 — [illegible] Battery R.F.A. — 932

Place	Date	Hour	Summary of Events and Information	Remarks and references to Appendices
[illegible]	[illegible]		[illegible] on new position [illegible]	
			Gunner W. Reynolds wounded	
			[illegible] [illegible] [illegible] to Hospital	
			Gunner Walker [illegible] from Hospital	

1875 Wt. W593/826 1,000,000 4/15 J.B.C. & A. A.D.S.S./Forms/C. 2118.

Instructions regarding War Diaries and Intelligence Summaries are contained in F. S. Regs., Part II. and the Staff Manual respectively. Title Pages will be prepared in manuscript.

WAR DIARY
or
INTELLIGENCE SUMMARY
(Erase heading not required.)

Army Form C. 2118

August 1916 — [illegible] Battery [illegible] — 933

Place	Date	Hour	Summary of Events and Information	Remarks and references to Appendices
			Moved [illegible] to new position N of Bernafay Wood. Had a [illegible] [illegible] as the road running along E edge of Bernafay Wood was [illegible] blocked with disabled transport. The Detachments had to [illegible] the road by hand. Got into action by 9 am. [illegible] wood and registered by 3.10 am on E end of GINCHY.	
			[illegible] was supposed to attack at 8 am but was put off owing to [illegible] weather.	
			[illegible] all day.	

1875 Wt. W593/826 1,000,000 4/15 J.B.C. & A. A.D.S.S./Forms/C. 2118.

Instructions regarding War Diaries and Intelligence Summaries are contained in F.S. Regs., Part II. and the Staff Manual respectively. Title Pages will be prepared in manuscript.

WAR DIARY
or
INTELLIGENCE SUMMARY
(Erase heading not required.)

Army Form C. 2118

934

Place	Date	Hour	Summary of Events and Information	Remarks and references to Appendices
[illegible]	[illegible]	[illegible]	Returned from [illegible]	
			Rained all day	
			[illegible] was shelled with 8" shells. No damage	
			[illegible] to Hospital	

1875 Wt. W593/826 1,000,000 4/15 J.B.C. & A. A.D.S.S./Forms/C. 2118.

Instructions regarding War Diaries and Intelligence Summaries are contained in F. S. Regs., Part II. and the Staff Manual respectively. Title Pages will be prepared in manuscript.

WAR DIARY
or
INTELLIGENCE SUMMARY
(Erase heading not required.)

Army Form C. 2118

August 1916 "W" Battery R.H.A. 935

Place	Date	Hour	Summary of Events and Information	Remarks and references to Appendices
[illegible]	[illegible]	10am	Battery was shelled with 8" shell } no damage	
		[illegible]		
			[illegible] think this was caused by the battery on our left having [illegible]	
			[illegible] all in a [illegible]	
			[illegible] all day, and everyone by this time was covered with mud	
			and dirt	
			[illegible] Commanding returned from Leave	

1875 Wt. W593/826 1,000,000 4/15 J.B.C. & A. A.D.S.S./Forms/C. 2118.

Instructions regarding War Diaries and Intelligence Summaries are contained in F.S. Regs., Part II. and the Staff Manual respectively. Title Pages will be prepared in manuscript.

Army Form C. 2118

936

WAR DIARY
or
INTELLIGENCE SUMMARY

(Erase heading not required.)

Place	Date	Hour	Summary of Events and Information	Remarks and references to Appendices
		4 pm	[illegible] but [illegible]	
			Dug outs at last position blown in by 12" shells and some of our signallers who were resting there were buried but got out untouched owing to them having had a shovel in the dug-out with them	
		5.30 pm	S. O. S.	
		During the night	Again shelled with Gas Shells.	

Field
11th Sept 1916

E Rich
Major R.H.A.
Cmdg "U" Battery R.H.A.

1875 Wt. W593/826 1,000,000 4/15 J.B.C. & A. A.D.S.S./Forms/C. 2118.

SERIAL NO. 273.

Confidential

War Diary

of

"U" Battery, Royal Horse Artillery.

FROM 1st September 1916 TO 30th September 1916

Army Form C. 2118

Instructions regarding War Diaries and Intelligence Summaries are contained in F. S. Regs., Part II. and the Staff Manual respectively. Title Pages will be prepared in manuscript.

WAR DIARY
or
INTELLIGENCE SUMMARY
(Erase heading not required.)

September 1916. "U" Battery RHA

Place	Date	Hour	Summary of Events and Information	Remarks and references to Appendices
N of Bernafay Wood.	1st	8am.	Shelled by 4" Gun Battery in enfilade. Active men cleared from position & we remained in a trench near by till 11 am when the enemy stopped shelling. On return found No 4 Gun (which belonged to 123 Bty RFA) has sustained a direct hit & was completely ruined.	
			A few Gas Shells in the afternoon.	
			*This was a bad day for us as we had 1 native driver & 6 horses killed & 3 men & 4 horses wounded, also a Gun knocked out.	
			*Drs Gathard and Wright wounded, and Indian Driver Lal Din killed	
			Sgt Nokes S. wounded but remained at duty	
			Gnr Melton H, Dr Callaghan J	
			" Nurse J, " Dutton W	
			" Peacock J, " Edwards H	
			" Fellbeam J, " Granger H	
			" Roberts J, " Harrison H	
			" Taylor A, " White W } Joined from 1st Ind Cav. Div Ammn Column	

Instructions regarding War Diaries and Intelligence Summaries are contained in F. S. Regs., Part II. and the Staff Manual respectively. Title Pages will be prepared in manuscript.

WAR DIARY
or
INTELLIGENCE SUMMARY

(Erase heading not required.)

Army Form C. 2118

September 1916. "U" Battery RHA

Place	Date	Hour	Summary of Events and Information	Remarks and references to Appendices
N of Bernafay wood.	2nd.		* Officers mess Cook wounded.	
		7.30 am.	All Guns registered.	
		8 am.	Preliminary bombardment commenced	
			"U" Bty shelled the orchard in GINCHY & 2 trenches just E of it.	
			*63353 Bomb^r Kitchenside C. to hospital Wounded.	

1875 Wt. W593/826 1,000,000 4/15 J.B.C. & A. A.D.S.S./Forms/C. 2118.

Instructions regarding War Diaries and Intelligence Summaries are contained in F. S. Regs., Part II. and the Staff Manual respectively. Title Pages will be prepared in manuscript.

WAR DIARY
or
INTELLIGENCE SUMMARY
(Erase heading not required.)

Army Form C. 2118

September 1916. "U" Battery R.H.A.

Place	Date	Hour	Summary of Events and Information	Remarks and references to Appendices
N of Bernafay Wood	3rd		Battle of GUILLEMONT & ~~GOUACH~~ GINCHY.	
			At 12 noon the infantry assaulted & at 12.45 Pm the Prisoners commenced to pass the Battery position.	
			Guillemont was captured & our infantry got as far as the outskirts of Ginchy.	
			About 3 Pm. an aeroplane reported the enemy massing in ALE ALLEY (NE of DELVILLE WOOD) the Battery was turned onto them.	
			When the firing was dying down & the men were carrying ammunition a High velocity Battery shelled the position leaving but luckily only the first shell caused casualties. The wounded were got down into the dugout after being ~~dressed~~ attended to in the open by several Subalterns & men who were exposed to heavy fire.	
			53509 Cpl Porter G killed.	
			50480 Bdr Peckham A } Wounded.	
			44510 Gunr Clarke R } Wounded.	
			62120 Luff A } Wounded.	

1875 Wt. W593/826 1,000,000 4/15 J.B.C. & A. A.D.S.S./Forms/C. 2118.

Instructions regarding War Diaries and Intelligence Summaries are contained in F. S. Regs., Part II. and the Staff Manual respectively. Title Pages will be prepared in manuscript.

WAR DIARY
or
INTELLIGENCE SUMMARY
(Erase heading not required.)

Army Form C. 2118

September 1916. "U" Battery R.H.A.

Place	Date	Hour	Summary of Events and Information	Remarks and references to Appendices
N of Bernafay Wood.	4th		Roman Strafe to clear a German Strong post out of ALE ALLEY.	

1875 Wt. W593/826 1,000,000 4/15 J.B.C. & A. A.D.S.S./Forms/C. 2118.

80

Army Form C. 2118

WAR DIARY
or
INTELLIGENCE SUMMARY
(Erase heading not required.)

Instructions regarding War Diaries and Intelligence Summaries are contained in F. S. Regs., Part II. and the Staff Manual respectively. Title Pages will be prepared in manuscript.

September 1916 "U" Battery R.H.A.

Place	Date	Hour	Summary of Events and Information	Remarks and references to Appendices
100x N of BERNAFAY WOOD.	5th	5am.	Relieved by 119 Battery RFA. – They took over our Guns which we were sad to leave as they were the original 6 the Battery had brought into action, one after having been blown up by an 8" the carriage destroyed, having been mounted on a new carriage. –	
			The Battery has fired 45,114 rounds whilst in action at the "Battle of the Somme" & having never had less than 5 Guns in action. At times they had had as many Guns in action as the rest of the Brigade put together. –	
			The men were almost entirely unaffected by their heavy casualties & the shelling they had been subjected to. –	
			No of rounds fired 35,699 Shrapnel – 9,415 HE = Total 45,114	
			Casualties – Officers Killed 2 wounded 4	
			Men – ~~8~~6 – 26	
			Horses. – 10 – 10	
			Guns – direct hits on. 2.	

1875 Wt. W593/826 1,000,000 4/15 J.B.C. & A. A.D.S.S./Forms/C. 2118.

Instructions regarding War Diaries and Intelligence Summaries are contained in F. S. Regs., Part II. and the Staff Manual respectively. Title Pages will be prepared in manuscript.

WAR DIARY
or
INTELLIGENCE SUMMARY

(Erase heading not required.)

September 1916. "U" Battery RHA.

Army Form C. 2118

Place	Date	Hour	Summary of Events and Information	Remarks and references to Appendices
BECORDEL.	5th	9am.	After a fearful journey, having to clear the road of abandoned wagons - wounded horses etc, the Battery arrived at the wagon line where Breakfast was got & the prepared to march	
LA NEULILLE.		11am.	Marched at head of 28th Bde RFA to LA NEUVILLE where the horses & vehicles were bivouaced in a field & the men billeted in a big barn.	

1875 Wt. W593/826 1,000,000 4/15 J.B.C. & A. A.D.S.S./Forms/C. 2118.

Army Form C. 2118

Instructions regarding War Diaries and Intelligence Summaries are contained in F. S. Regs., Part II. and the Staff Manual respectively. Title Pages will be prepared in manuscript.

WAR DIARY
or
INTELLIGENCE SUMMARY

(Erase heading not required.)

September 1916. "U" Battery R.H.A.

Place	Date	Hour	Summary of Events and Information	Remarks and references to Appendices
LA NEUVILLE	6th		Cleaning up & overhauling. The mud on the wagons was so bad that they had to be soaked in the river & then the mud chipped off.	

1875 Wt. W593/826 1,000,000 4/15 J.B.C. & A. A.D.S.S./Forms/C. 2118.

Army Form C. 2118

Instructions regarding War Diaries and Intelligence Summaries are contained in F. S. Regs., Part II. and the Staff Manual respectively. Title Pages will be prepared in manuscript.

WAR DIARY
or
INTELLIGENCE SUMMARY

September 1916. *(Erase heading not required.)* "U" Battery R.H.A.

Place	Date	Hour	Summary of Events and Information	Remarks and references to Appendices
LA NEUVILLE	4th		Maj General Budworth CRA. 4th Army sent for Major Rich as he knew him & wished to hear about the Battery.	

1875 Wt. W593/826 1,000,000 4/15 J.B.C. & A. A.D.S.S./Forms/C. 2118.

Army Form C. 2118

Instructions regarding War Diaries and Intelligence Summaries are contained in F. S. Regs., Part II. and the Staff Manual respectively. Title Pages will be prepared in manuscript.

WAR DIARY
or
INTELLIGENCE SUMMARY

September 8th 1916. *(Erase heading not required.)* U Battery R.H.A.

Place	Date	Hour	Summary of Events and Information	Remarks and references to Appendices
LA NEUVILLE	8th		New Promotions to fill vacancies &c – Gun Stores overhauled.	

1875 Wt. W593/826 1,000,000 4/15 J.B.C. & A. A.D.S.S./Forms/C. 2118.

Army Form C. 2118

Instructions regarding War Diaries and Intelligence Summaries are contained in F. S. Regs., Part II. and the Staff Manual respectively. Title Pages will be prepared in manuscript.

WAR DIARY
or
INTELLIGENCE SUMMARY
(Erase heading not required.)

September 1916. "U" Battery R.H.A.

Place	Date	Hour	Summary of Events and Information	Remarks and references to Appendices
LA NEUVILLE	9th		Drill order parade with the Battery Staff	
			H.T. Batteries lying near were visited –	
			Bdr Trowell 6 to Hospital	

1875 Wt. W593/826 1,000,000 4/15 J.B.C. & A. A.D.S.S./Forms/C. 2118.

Instructions regarding War Diaries and Intelligence Summaries are contained in F. S. Regs., Part II. and the Staff Manual respectively. Title Pages will be prepared in manuscript.

Army Form C. 2118

WAR DIARY
or
INTELLIGENCE SUMMARY
(Erase heading not required.)

September 1916. "U" Battery R H A

Place	Date	Hour	Summary of Events and Information	Remarks and references to Appendices
LA NEUVILLE	10th	2pm.	Officers parade in detached Section duties.	
			B.S.M. Brixey returned to the "Chestnut Troop" owing to an adverse report.	
			Saddler Andrews J. to Hospital	
			Bombr Bentham and 1 riding horse rejoined 1st Ind Cav Ammn Column.	

1875 Wt. W593/826 1,000,000 4/15 J.B.C. & A. A.D.S.S./Forms/C. 2118.

Instructions regarding War Diaries and Intelligence Summaries are contained in F. S. Regs., Part II. and the Staff Manual respectively. Title Pages will be prepared in manuscript.

WAR DIARY
or
INTELLIGENCE SUMMARY
(Erase heading not required.)

September 1916. "U" Battery R.H.A.

Army Form C. 2118

Place	Date	Hour	Summary of Events and Information	Remarks and references to Appendices
LA NEUVILLE	11th.			
	12th		Bomb.r Durben R. to Hospital	
	13th		Battery Staff parade.	
			Driver Steward to Hospital	

Army Form C. 2118

Instructions regarding War Diaries and Intelligence Summaries are contained in F. S. Regs., Part II. and the Staff Manual respectively. Title Pages will be prepared in manuscript.

WAR DIARY
or
INTELLIGENCE SUMMARY

(Erase heading not required.)

September 1916. "U" Battery R.H.A.

Place	Date	Hour	Summary of Events and Information	Remarks and references to Appendices
LA NEUVILLE	14th		Drill order parade with whole Battery. Good country.	
			28th Bde RFA made the Battery complete with 6 Guns as we had only had one before. All new except one.	
			Heard "A" & "Q" were approaching so B.C. rode over to see them at QUERRIEUX.	
			Received orders late at night that "A" & "Q" would pick up "U" at 5.45 am next morning —	
			Gunners Fryer ? and Valentine W. in Guard Room.	

1875 Wt. W593/826 1,000,000 4/15 J.B.C. & A. A.D.S.S./Forms/C. 2118.

Instructions regarding War Diaries and Intelligence Summaries are contained in F. S. Regs., Part II. and the Staff Manual respectively. Title Pages will be prepared in manuscript.

WAR DIARY or INTELLIGENCE SUMMARY

(Erase heading not required.)

Army Form C. 2118

September 1916. "W" Battery R.H.A.

Place	Date	Hour	Summary of Events and Information	Remarks and references to Appendices
LA NEUVILLE	15th	5.45am	Marched with rest of 1st Indian H.Q. Bde to VILLE SUR ANCRE	
VILLE-SUR-ANCRE		8am.	On 1½ hours notice to move up to the line –	
			Cpl Cldrington awarded the Military Medal.	
VILLE-SUR-ANCRE	16th		Still waiting	
			2 Draught Horses to M.V.S. Sialkote Cavalry Brigade	
			2 Draught Horses to Jodhpur Lancers	
			1 Draught Horse to Military Police 1st Ind Cav Division	
			1 Draught Horse to Hdqrs 1st Ind Cav Divn	
			10 Draught Horses joined from Remount Depot.	
			Driver Steward J from Hospital	
			A/Bdr Hicken and one horse attached from Divl Ammn Column.	

Army Form C. 2118

Instructions regarding War Diaries and Intelligence Summaries are contained in F. S. Regs., Part II. and the Staff Manual respectively. Title Pages will be prepared in manuscript.

WAR DIARY
or
INTELLIGENCE SUMMARY

September 1916. (*Erase heading not required.*) "U" Battery RHA

Place	Date	Hour	Summary of Events and Information	Remarks and references to Appendices
VILLE-SUR-ANCRE	14th		B.C. went with Lt Col Charlton RHA to show him the ground round Montauban. Rain.	
"	18th		Capt H.W. HUGGINS D.S.O. awarded the Military Cross. – Rain all day. No cover except 4 tents & the wagon covers. Driver Steward J to Hospital Indian Driver George Khan to Hospital.	

Instructions regarding War Diaries and Intelligence Summaries are contained in F. S. Regs., Part II. and the Staff Manual respectively. Title Pages will be prepared in manuscript.

WAR DIARY
or
INTELLIGENCE SUMMARY
(Erase heading not required.)

Army Form C. 2118

September 1916. "U" Battery R.H.A.

Place	Date	Hour	Summary of Events and Information	Remarks and references to Appendices
VILLE-SUR-ANCRE	19th		B.C. went in a car with Col Cmdg H.A. Bde. to BERNAFAY WOOD & walked to GINCHY – DELVILLE WOOD RIDGE & on to Ridge N. of it which dominates LESBOEUFS & GUEUDECOURT – Rain all morning.	
			Lance Naick Nawab Khan rejoined from Hospital	
"	20th		Draught Horse No 101 to M.V.S. Sialkote Cavalry Brigade.	
			Dr Matthews J. returned from leave.	
			L/Naick Mohamed Khan. } Ind Dr Jaswant Singh. } Recruit Ram Saran } Joined from Indian Base Depot Marseilles	
			Bombr Whitehead W. rejoined Divl Ammn Column.	

1875 Wt. W593/826 1,000,000 4/15 J.B.C. & A. A.D.S.S./Forms/C. 2118.

Army Form C. 2118

Instructions regarding War Diaries and Intelligence Summaries are contained in F. S. Regs., Part II. and the Staff Manual respectively. Title Pages will be prepared in manuscript.

WAR DIARY
or
INTELLIGENCE SUMMARY
(Erase heading not required.)

September 1916. "U" Battery R.H.A.

Place	Date	Hour	Summary of Events and Information	Remarks and references to Appendices
VILLE-SUR-ANCRE	21st		Rain. Gunner Field R to Hospital. 3 Draught Horses to M.V.S. Lucknow Cavalry Brigade.	
	22nd		B.C. went with Bde Cmdr R.A. – O.C. "A" & O.C. "Q" rode to N end of Bernafay Wood – Walked W of LONGUEVAL to ridge which over looks Flers – Then to N of Delville Wood & looked at LIGNY-THILLOY "B" Coghlan awarded the D.C.M. 1 Draught Horse to M.V.S. Sialkote Brigade 63353 Bombr Kitchenside C rejoined from Base Havre. 12128 Bombr Phillips J.R. attached from Base Havre.	

1875 Wt. W593/826 1,000,000 4/15 J.B.C. & A. A.D.S.S./Forms/C. 2118.

Army Form C. 2118

WAR DIARY
or
INTELLIGENCE SUMMARY
(Erase heading not required.)

Instructions regarding War Diaries and Intelligence Summaries are contained in F. S. Regs., Part II. and the Staff Manual respectively. Title Pages will be prepared in manuscript.

September 1916

"U" Battery. R.H.A.

Place	Date	Hour	Summary of Events and Information	Remarks and references to Appendices
VILLE-SUR-ANCRE	23rd		Div order [illegible] whole Battery.	
			Rev Gibbons C.F. lectures to the Battery on Poitiers & Joan of Arc.	
"	24th		Received orders to march next morning.	
			Received from G.O.C. RA 5 Div an excellent report on work of "U" whilst attached to them.	
			Air Mechanic Donovan and one Wireless set attached from R.F. Corps.	

1875 Wt. W593/826 1,000,000 4/15 J.B.C. & A. A.D.S.S./Forms/C. 2118.

Army Form C. 2118

Instructions regarding War Diaries and Intelligence Summaries are contained in F. S. Regs., Part II. and the Staff Manual respectively. Title Pages will be prepared in manuscript.

WAR DIARY
or
INTELLIGENCE SUMMARY

(Erase heading not required.)

September 1916. "W" Battery. R.H.A.

Place	Date	Hour	Summary of Events and Information	Remarks and references to Appendices
VILLE-SUR-ANCRE	25th	6.30am.	Marched.	
MAMETZ	"	9am.	arrived – B.C. went to Colonel at Montauban but no chance of Gapping as a strong German post between Gueudecourt & Lesboeufs held on. This was on our line of advance unfortunately so we couldn't start.	
		9.P.m.	Got orders to march back to Ville-Sur Ancre at 9.45 P.m. Delayed for 1½ hours by "Q" Bty who got stuck.	
	9			

1875 Wt. W593/826 1,000,000 4/15 J.B.C. & A. A.D.S.S./Forms/C. 2118.

Instructions regarding War Diaries and Intelligence Summaries are contained in F. S. Regs., Part II. and the Staff Manual respectively. Title Pages will be prepared in manuscript.

Army Form C. 2118

WAR DIARY
or
INTELLIGENCE SUMMARY

(Erase heading not required.)

September 1916. "U" Battery R.H.A.

Place	Date	Hour	Summary of Events and Information	Remarks and references to Appendices
VILLE-SUR-ANCRE	26th	1am.	Arrived & found camp has been bombed that evening.	
		2.P.m.	Received message from Lucknow Bde "Attached to us - Saddle up at once"	
MAMETZ.		4P.m.	B.C. in Car with Brig Gen Lucknow Cav Bde to Montauban - Bty started at 4.20 Pm & marched to Mametz. Guedecourt finally taken but the Lucknow Bde were not employed.	

Army Form C. 2118

Instructions regarding War Diaries and Intelligence Summaries are contained in F. S. Regs., Part II. and the Staff Manual respectively. Title Pages will be prepared in manuscript.

WAR DIARY
or
INTELLIGENCE SUMMARY
(Erase heading not required.)

September 1916. "U" Battery. R.H.A.

Place	Date	Hour	Summary of Events and Information	Remarks and references to Appendices
MAMETZ	24th	9am	marched.	
VILLE-SUR-ANCRE		noon	Arrived & has dinners.	
		2Pm.	marched.	
BUISSY.		6.30Pm	Arrived & bivouacked - Very heavy thunderstorms - "N" Bty RHA has heard of us coming & has tea ready for the whole battery -	

1875 Wt. W593/826 1,000,000 4/15 J.B.C. & A. A.D.S.S./Forms/C. 2118.

Army Form C. 2118

WAR DIARY
or
INTELLIGENCE SUMMARY
(Erase heading not required.)

Instructions regarding War Diaries and Intelligence Summaries are contained in F. S. Regs., Part II. and the Staff Manual respectively. Title Pages will be prepared in manuscript.

September 1916. "U" Battery RHA

Place	Date	Hour	Summary of Events and Information	Remarks and references to Appendices
BUISSY.	28th	8. am	Marched thro Amiens where B.C. reported for interfering with A.P.M. who tried to cut Bty in ½.	
CROUY		1 Pm.	Arrived after a hot march of very bad march discipline by whole Division —	
			1 Draught Horse to M.V.S. Lucknow Cavalry Brigade	
CROUY	29th	7.30 am	Marched	
EAUCOURT.		Noon	Arrived. Rained most of the way.	
			Gr Abbott J. to Hospital	

1875 Wt. W593/826 1,000,000 4/15 J.B.C. & A. A.D.S.S./Forms/C. 2118.

Army Form C. 2118

Instructions regarding War Diaries and Intelligence Summaries are contained in F. S. Regs., Part II. and the Staff Manual respectively. Title Pages will be prepared in manuscript.

WAR DIARY
or
INTELLIGENCE SUMMARY
(Erase heading not required.)

September 1916. "U" Battery R.H.A.

Place	Date	Hour	Summary of Events and Information	Remarks and references to Appendices
EAUCOURT	30th	4.30 am	Marched thro Abbeville & Crecy Forest.	
ROSSIGNOL		12.30 pm	Arrived after a good march. but as these were to be our rest billets we were very disappointed as they were very bad. & water 1½ miles away. Went to Crecy to try & fix up others	

Field
4-10-1916

C Rich
Major R.H.A.
Cmdg "U" Battery R.H.A.

1875 Wt. W593/826 1,000,000 4/15 J.B.C. & A. A.D.S.S./Forms/C. 2118.

SERIAL NO. 273.

Confidential

War Diary

of

"U" Battery, Royal Horse Artillery

FROM 1st October 1916 TO ~~31st October~~ 30th November 1916.

1

Army Form C. 2118.

WAR DIARY or INTELLIGENCE SUMMARY

(Erase heading not required.)

Instructions regarding War Diaries and Intelligence Summaries are contained in F. S. Regs., Part II. and the Staff Manual respectively. Title Pages will be prepared in manuscript.

October 1916 — "U" Battery. R.H.A.

Place	Date	Hour	Summary of Events and Information	Remarks and references to Appendices
	1st.		Report on Work of Battery whilst with 15th Corps. July 18 – Sept 4. 1916.	
			O.C. "U" Battery. R.H.A.	
			The Lt Col. Commanding the Brigade has great pleasure in forwarding the attached highly satisfactory reports. They reflect great credit on Majors Lascelles and Rich and all Officers, N.C.O's and men of the Battery. They are in accordance with the highest traditions of the Royal Horse Artillery, which the Lt Col. Commanding is convinced every battery in the Brigade will always maintain. These reports to be read out on parade by batteries and the D.A. Column.	
			S/d L. E. Westrope. for R.H.A. for Adjt. R.H.A. Brigade.	
			24-9-1916	
			"U" Battery R.H.A.	
			Joined 5th Division at HEILLY 18th July 1916, and were allotted to 28th Brigade R.F.A. to take place of 122nd Battery (Third Army School Battery). Went into action 20th July 1916 just S.E. of MONTAUBAN commanded by Major Lascelles.	

Contd.

2449 Wt. W14957/M90 750,000 1/16 J.B.C. & A. Forms/C.2118/12.

1

Instructions regarding War Diaries and Intelligence Summaries are contained in F. S. Regs., Part II. and the Staff Manual respectively. Title Pages will be prepared in manuscript.

Army Form C. 2118.

WAR DIARY
or
INTELLIGENCE SUMMARY
(Erase heading not required.)

October 1916 "U" Battery R.H.A.

Place	Date	Hour	Summary of Events and Information	Remarks and references to Appendices
	1st.		Remained in Action until Sept 4th (When they went into rest at LA NEUVILLE with the 28th Brigade R.F.A). For the last part of the time the battery was commanded by Major E E Rich. Whilst they were in action, besides doing the ordinary work of the Brigade they had a forward gun S.W of LONGUEVAL, at the end of July, which did very useful work enfilading WOOD LANE during the attacks by the 5th Division. 2/Lieut W.H Holmes did very well on this occasion. A forward Section N of BERNAFAY WOOD did good work wire cutting on HOP ALLEY before the 14th Division attack on August 18th. Capt H W Huggins D.S.O. carried out a particularly valuable reconnaissance round DELVILLE WOOD and established an OP from which much of the fire of the Brigade was observed. (He was recommended for the Military Cross for this work). 2/Lieut Clark-Williams also did a very good reconnaissance in connection with the attack on BEER TRENCH and ZZ TRENCH on August 18th, going into a disused German Sap and obtaining useful information. The total casualties whilst the Battery were in action were :- 2 Officers killed, 4 Officers wounded; 6 Other ranks killed, 26 Other ranks wounded; 10 Horses killed, 10 ~~Horses~~ wounded. The Group Commander (Lt Col Harding Newman) spoke very highly of the battery and said that whenever a difficult or dangerous bit of work had to be done, "U" Battery were certain to volunteer for it. S/d S. Gore Browne. Major R.H.A Brigade Major 5th Div^l Arty. 14-9-1916	Cont^d

2449 Wt. W14957/M90 750,000 1/16 J.B.C. & A. Forms/C.2118/12.

Army Form C. 2118.

Instructions regarding War Diaries and Intelligence Summaries are contained in F. S. Regs., Part II. and the Staff Manual respectively. Title Pages will be prepared in manuscript.

WAR DIARY or INTELLIGENCE SUMMARY

(Erase heading not required.)

October 1916 "U" Battery R H A

Place	Date	Hour	Summary of Events and Information	Remarks and references to Appendices
	1st.		G.O.C. Cavalry Corps. I attach the report of the G.O.C. 5th Div Arty on the splendid work done by "U" Battery R H A whilst serving with the XV Corps. I always expect something above the average from the R H A and it is a great pleasure to me to be able to assure you that this battery has well maintained the high reputation borne by that branch of the Royal Regiment of Artillery. I shall be grateful if you will express to Major Cavellier, Major Rich, and the Officers, N C O's and men of "U" Battery R H A my appreciation of their efforts. 19-9-1916 Sd. T H Horne Lieut Genl. Commanding XV Corps 1st Indian Cavalry Division In forwarding the attached report, the G O C Cavalry Corps wishes the contents of the same to be communicated to the Officers, N C O's and men concerned, and wishes to congratulate them himself for the fine work they have done. Cavalry Corps. No G 31 d/- 23-9-1916 Sd D Baird Major for Brig Genl. Gen Staff. 1st Indian R H A Brigade The Divisional Commander has great pleasure in forwarding these highly complimentary reports, and suggests that the whole Brigade be made acquainted with their contents 1st Ind Cav Divn Sd. C A C Godwin Lt Col G 9/2. d/- 24-9-16 Genl. Staff.	

2449 Wt. W14957/M90 750,000 1/16 J.B.C. & A. Forms/C.2118/12.

Instructions regarding War Diaries and Intelligence Summaries are contained in F. S. Regs., Part II. and the Staff Manual respectively. Title Pages will be prepared in manuscript.

Army Form C. 2118.

WAR DIARY
or
INTELLIGENCE SUMMARY
(Erase heading not required.)

October 1916 — U Battery R.H.A.

Place	Date	Hour	Summary of Events and Information	Remarks and references to Appendices
ROSIGNOL	~~1st~~ 1st		marched to CRECY to billets at ROSIGNOL were very bad and there was no water nearer than 1½ miles. Driver Fulford to Hosp^l. Gunner Maas to Hosp^l.	
CRECY.	2nd		Heavy Rain	
CRECY	3rd		Heavy Rain. Light Draught Horses No. 430, 312, 195, to Mobile Vety Section, Lucknow Cavalry Brigade. 22519 Corp^l Adams admonished. Driver J.E. Hill awarded 14 days F.P. No. 1.	

2449 Wt. W14957/M90 750,000 1/16 J.B.C. & A. Forms/C.2118/12.

Army Form C. 2118.

Instructions regarding War Diaries and Intelligence Summaries are contained in F. S. Regs., Part II. and the Staff Manual respectively. Title Pages will be prepared in manuscript.

WAR DIARY
or
INTELLIGENCE SUMMARY

(Erase heading not required.)

October 1916 "N" Battery R.H.A.

Place	Date	Hour	Summary of Events and Information	Remarks and references to Appendices
CRECY	~~[illegible]~~ 4th		D.A.D.R. came round and cast 4 horses and handed 6 over to the Lucknow Cav Bde all very thin and old. So did a very good stroke of work. Gr Edwards rejoined from Base Havre.	
CRECY	5th		Field-day with Lucknow Cav. Bde round Forest l'Abbaye. Light Draught Horses Nos 380. 287 transferred to 36th Jacobs Horse. " " " 293. 438 " 1st (Kings) Dragoon Guards 1 unnumbered and 434 " 29th Lancers.	
CRECY	6th		Conference at R.H.A. Bde Office on training Etc. Discussed 13 pr versus 18 pr and on result put in to have our 18 pr's changed for 13 pr's Driver Fulford rejoined from Hospital.	

2449 Wt. W14957/M90 750,000 1/16 J.B.C. & A. Forms/C.2118/12.

Instructions regarding War Diaries and Intelligence Summaries are contained in F. S. Regs., Part II. and the Staff Manual respectively. Title Pages will be prepared in manuscript.

Army Form C. 2118.

WAR DIARY
or
INTELLIGENCE SUMMARY
(Erase heading not required.)

October 1916 "U" Battery R.H.A.

Place	Date	Hour	Summary of Events and Information	Remarks and references to Appendices
CRECY.	~~2nd~~ 4th		Field-day with Lucknow Cav Bde round country between Crecy Forrest and mouth of R. Somme. Troops showed improvement and were not so wild. 2. Remounts joined from Remount Depot. Light Draught Horses Nos 182, 100, 101, 142, to M.V.S. Lucknow Cav. Bde. Gunner Foster J to Hospl.	
CRECY.	8th	4.30PM	Lecture, by Rev. Gibbons C.F. to 1st Indian Cav Div, on Battle of Crecy: lecture delivered standing on the actual spot where King Edward watched the Battle from.	
CRECY.	9th		Divisional Inspection of Lucknow Cav Bde doing a Gapping scheme.	

2449 Wt. W14957/M90 750,000 1/16 J.B.C. & A. Forms/C.2118/12.

Army Form C. 2118.

Instructions regarding War Diaries and Intelligence Summaries are contained in F. S. Regs., Part II. and the Staff Manual respectively. Title Pages will be prepared in manuscript.

WAR DIARY
or
INTELLIGENCE SUMMARY
(Erase heading not required.)

October 1916 — N Battery R.H.A.

Place	Date	Hour	Summary of Events and Information	Remarks and references to Appendices
CRECY.	~~Oct 9th~~ 10th		Horse No 4.411 to Hdqrs. Lucknow Cav Bde.	
CRECY	11th	9 a.m.	Did Lapping Scheme in skeleton with Sergeants.	
		11 a.m.	Officers went hunting with the Crecy Forest Boar Hounds. Hounds are leggy foxhounds. Found a boar but did not have much of a hunt as hounds had not hunted for 27 years and were not fit and would not draw or cast.	
CRECY	12th		Lieut Cowling took his section on a Field-day	
			13 Remounts came, quite the very best lot ever seen. One died of fever directly it arrived but the others are a splendid lot.	
			Gunr. F Abbott rejoined from Hospl.	
			Br. Durbin rejoined from Base Havre.	

2449 Wt. W14957/M90 750,000 1/16 J.B.C. & A. Forms/C.2118/12.

1

Instructions regarding War Diaries and Intelligence Summaries are contained in F. S. Regs., Part II. and the Staff Manual respectively. Title Pages will be prepared in manuscript.

WAR DIARY
or
INTELLIGENCE SUMMARY
(Erase heading not required.)

Army Form C. 2118.

October 1916 — "U" Battery R.H.A.

Place	Date	Hour	Summary of Events and Information	Remarks and references to Appendices
CRECY.	~~30th~~ 13th		Field-day round Crecy with Lucknow Cav. Bde. Gunner Pilbeam J (Commissioned) Transferred to 20th Field Ambulance for Duty as Dental Surgeon. Br. R. Hickin rejoined Ammunition Column.	
CRECY.	14th		Sergt. Child B., Yates R., A/Br. Harris, Amt S.Sgt. Willis } awarded "Military Medal". Indian Driver Fateh Jang awarded the 2nd Class of Indian Order of Merit. 1 Remount Died. Driver Wren G to Hosp.	
	15th	10 a.m.	Officers went out selecting positions for Laying Saturations.	

2449 Wt. W14957/M90 750,000 1/16 J.B.C. & A. Forms/C.2118/12.

Instructions regarding War Diaries and Intelligence Summaries are contained in F. S. Regs., Part II. and the Staff Manual respectively. Title Pages will be prepared in manuscript.

Army Form C. 2118.

WAR DIARY
or
INTELLIGENCE SUMMARY
(Erase heading not required.)

October 1916 — N Battery R.H.A.

Place	Date	Hour	Summary of Events and Information	Remarks and references to Appendices
CRECY	~~[illegible]~~ 16	5.30 PM	Conference at Divl. H. Qrs on umpiring on the coming Field-day	
CRECY	17th		Field-day with Lucknow Cav Bde. round Argentillers. Received warning that R H A Bde would probably march on the 19th.	
CRECY	18th	6 a.m	Major and Captain got up at 6 a.m. as they were to go umpiring on a Field-day, but just starting it was cancelled.	
		11.30 a.m	General Lengman. C. R A. Cav. Corps. Came round the horses and said they were looking very well. Packing up to move. 28430 Saddler Hawkes T. J. Joined from Ammunition Column. Corpl. Thornley to Hosp?	

2449 Wt. W14957/M90 750,000 1/16 J.B.C. & A. Forms/C.2118/12.

1

Instructions regarding War Diaries and Intelligence Summaries are contained in F. S. Regs., Part II. and the Staff Manual respectively. Title Pages will be prepared in manuscript.

WAR DIARY
or
INTELLIGENCE SUMMARY
(Erase heading not required.)

Army Form C. 2118.

October 1916 — "U" Battery R.H.A.

Place	Date	Hour	Summary of Events and Information	Remarks and references to Appendices
CRECY	~~18th~~ 19th	9.45 a.m.	Marched 15 miles to NOEUX. Poor billets in a small village. "A" & "Q" Batteries in the same place. Very heavy rain at commencement of march. Sgt Child left for the 1st Army & R.A. School to be B.S.M. The Ammunition Column did not accompany the Brigade as some of it's horses had "Pinkeye". Horse No 424 to M.V.S. Lucknow. Cav. Bde.	
NOEUX	20th	9 a.m.	Marched with R.H.A. Brigade to HAVERNAS 18 miles to good billets. Horses still in the open. A very cold East wind which made it very bad for the Horses.	
HAVERNAS	21st	10 a.m.	Heard that as our Column had not come with us we were no use for the coming operations, and so should be sent back again.	
		6 P.M.	Warned to be ready to march back again.	

1		WAR DIARY or INTELLIGENCE SUMMARY				Army Form C. 2118.

Instructions regarding War Diaries and Intelligence Summaries are contained in F. S. Regs., Part II. and the Staff Manual respectively. Title Pages will be prepared in manuscript.

WAR DIARY
or
INTELLIGENCE SUMMARY
(Erase heading not required.)

October 1916 — N Battery R.H.A.

Place	Date	Hour	Summary of Events and Information	Remarks and references to Appendices
HAVERNAS.	~~[illegible]~~ 22nd	9.15 a.m.	Received order to march.	
		10.30 a.m.	Marched.	
		4.30 p.m.	Arrived at CRECY after a good march 24 miles	
		10. p.m.	Br Brodie, Br Fowler, Br. Rose. Gunner Randall and Driver Lowe. were found in a private house by the Military Police. One policeman lost his head and fired his revolver into the room and killed Driver Lowe.	
CRECY.	23rd	3 P.M.	Court of inquiry on Death of Driver Lowe.	
			Gunner Fitzgerald to Hosp^l.	
			1 Light Draught Horse joined from Remount Depot.	
			Gunner Forsythe proceeded on leave to United Kingdom.	
CRECY	24th	4 P.M.	Funeral of Driver Lowe in Crecy Cemetery.	
			Dr Callagan proceeded on leave to the United Kingdom.	
			Horse #20 died.	
			51229 ^aBr Fowler H. reverted to Driver. 52833 ^sgBr. Rose S. reverted to Driver. 84441 Gunner Randall J. awarded 14 dys F.P. No I	
			Sgt Child. admitted to Hosp^l whilst on the way to 1st Army R.A. school.	
			2 Lieut St J. Kemm ~~to~~ on leave to the United Kingdom	

Army Form C. 2118.

Instructions regarding War Diaries and Intelligence Summaries are contained in F. S. Regs., Part II. and the Staff Manual respectively. Title Pages will be prepared in manuscript.

WAR DIARY
or
INTELLIGENCE SUMMARY
(Erase heading not required.)

October 1916 — U Battery R.H.A.

Place	Date	Hour	Summary of Events and Information	Remarks and references to Appendices
CRECY	~~24th~~ 25th		Rain all day. Gunner Lansley on leave to the United Kingdom.	
CRECY.	26th	9 a.m.	Rain. Captain H.W. Huggins Interpreter d'Esterno and a party went to OCHANCOURT on a billetting reconnaissance as we are reported to be going there for winter billets. Driver Fulford on leave to the United Kingdom. Gunner Stanley and Driver White to Hosp?.	
CRECY.	27th	3 p.m.	Rain - Billetting Party returned.	
		3.30 p.m.	Hear we shall probably not go to Ochancourt after all. Gunner Mayes E. on leave to United Kingdom. Horse No. 391 Died. Driver Browning W. To Hosp?.	

2449 Wt. W14957/M90 750,000 1/16 J.B.C. & A. Forms/C.2118/12.

Army Form C. 2118.

WAR DIARY
or
INTELLIGENCE SUMMARY
(Erase heading not required.)

Instructions regarding War Diaries and Intelligence Summaries are contained in F. S. Regs., Part II. and the Staff Manual respectively. Title Pages will be prepared in manuscript.

October 1916 — U Battery RHA

Place	Date	Hour	Summary of Events and Information	Remarks and references to Appendices
CRECY.	31		Copy of Recommendations for awards Granted to "U" Battery RHA. Captain H.W. Huggins D.S.O. Awarded "Military Cross" For repeated outstanding gallantry under heavy shell fire notably when observing on 29-7-16. when he stuck to the remains of his O.P after it had been twice obliterated by shell fire, & again in steadying teams and drivers on 31-7-16 when ammunition was arriving and the guns under fire, this at great risk from plunging horses as well as from shell fire, His coolness & courage always had the greatest effect in steadying men. No. 29 1073 Arm. Staff Sergt W.E. Willis A.O.C attached "U" Battery RHA. Awarded "Military Medal" For gallantry & devotion to duty. During the 4 weeks this battery was in action it fired 45,000 rounds and when it came out of action its 6 original guns were in perfect condition. This was due to the devotion of duty displayed by S.S. Willis under the most trying circumstances. At all hours of the day and night he was to be seen working on the gun. He was continually subjected to very heavy shell fire whilst doing his work.	

2449 Wt. W14957/M90 750,000 1/16 J.B.C. & A. Forms/C.2118/12.

Instructions regarding War Diaries and Intelligence Summaries are contained in F. S. Regs., Part II. and the Staff Manual respectively. Title Pages will be prepared in manuscript.

WAR DIARY
or
INTELLIGENCE SUMMARY
(Erase heading not required.)

Army Form C. 2118.

October 1916 "U" Battery R.H.A.

Place	Date	Hour	Summary of Events and Information	Remarks and references to Appendices
CRECY.	~~27th~~ 28th		Court-martial on Br. Brodie. Heavy rain all day. Sgt. Crowhurst on leave to United Kingdom. Dr. W. White ~~from~~ to Hosp^l. Dr. Simms and Gr. Roberts to Hosp^l. 87692 Br. J Brodie reduced to the ranks by F.G.C.M.	
CRECY	29th		No 49013. Br. Durbin R.E. } No. 66436. Gr. W Woolgar } Awarded Military Medal.	
CRECY.	30th		Parade of Battery Staff. Gr Coles. leave to United Kingdom. Dr. White to Hosp^l. One Light Draught Horse. to M. V. S. Lucknow Cav. Bde. 28430 Saddl. Hawkes awarded 28 dys F.P. No. I.	
CRECY.	31st		Map Reading Etc. Gr Cartwright. leave to United Kingdom. Br. Phillips to Hosp^l. Dr. Simms rejoins from Hosp^l.	

1/11/16.

E Rich
Major RHA
Cmdg "U" Battery RHA.

Army Form C. 2118.

Instructions regarding War Diaries and Intelligence Summaries are contained in F. S. Regs., Part II. and the Staff Manual respectively. Title Pages will be prepared in manuscript.

WAR DIARY or INTELLIGENCE SUMMARY

(Erase heading not required.)

October 1916 — U Battery RHA

Place	Date	Hour	Summary of Events and Information	Remarks and references to Appendices
CRECY	31.		III. No 47516 Sergt. R.S. Yates. Awarded "Military Medal" For conspicuous courage and ability at all times. He performed on Officers' duties for a week from 22nd July with marked success, & generally made himself indispensable to the battery. He appears quite indifferent to any hostile fire and his alertness and quick wittedness are no less worthy of reward than the high courage and example he invariably shows.	

Instructions regarding War Diaries and Intelligence Summaries are contained in F. S. Regs., Part II. and the Staff Manual respectively. Title Pages will be prepared in manuscript.

WAR DIARY
or
INTELLIGENCE SUMMARY
(Erase heading not required.)

Army Form C. 2118.

October 1916 — W Battery RHA

Place	Date	Hour	Summary of Events and Information	Remarks and references to Appendices
October 1916			IV No. 37731 Sergt. Edgar. Burlingham Child. For repeated gallantry and outstanding ability in his own work. and that of F.O.O. which he frequently performed especially on 24th July 16 when he continued. to observe. in a bad barrage. after he had been buried in his. O.P. and F.O.O. of other batteries had left it. and taken cover. Awarded "Military Medal" 1st. Ind. Cav Divn order of. 14-10-16.	
			V 34960 Driver (BDr) Fredrick. Harris Awarded. Military Medal.	
			VI 1394 Indian Driver Fateh Jang Awarded "Indian Order of Merit" 2nd class 1st Ind Cav. Divn order of. 14-10-16. For gallantry and devotion to duty. 50,000 rounds of ammunition were brought up to the guns line and the battery had. forward. sections on 3 occasions To bring up this amount. of ammunition entailed the drivers being heavily shelled. Owing to the heavy casualties to the Officers it was impossible to detail individual acts which must have occurred. during such a long period. Their casualties 1 Driver and 10 horses killed. and 5 Drivers and 10 horses wounded. show what gallantry & devotion was displayed.	

Army Form C. 2118.

Instructions regarding War Diaries and Intelligence Summaries are contained in F. S. Regs., Part II. and the Staff Manual respectively. Title Pages will be prepared in manuscript.

WAR DIARY
or
INTELLIGENCE SUMMARY
(Erase heading not required.)

October 1916 — "U" Battery R.H.A.

Place	Date	Hour	Summary of Events and Information	Remarks and references to Appendices
October. 1916.	[illegible]		VII/63094 Br. William Creighton Awarded "D. C. M."	
			For extreme gallantry and devotion to duty. On 1 Sept. 1916 when 4 wagons were returning through MONTAUBAN after delivering Ammn. at the Gun Position, the enemy opened heavy Howitzer Barrage. The first shell killed 3 horses & wounded all three drivers of one team. Br. Creighton who was in charge, immediately gave orders to the 3 remaining wagons to go on and himself remained with the disabled wagon. As he was dressing one of the drivers another shell killed the other 3 horses and the centre driver. Br. Creighton continued dressing the remaining two men & then carried them to the dressing station. He then went back & collected the harness off the dead Horses before rejoining his unit	
			Had a second shell not obtained a direct hit on the team so quickly after the first one he would undoubtedly saved the lives of all team drivers	

Instructions regarding War Diaries and Intelligence Summaries are contained in F. S. Regs., Part II. and the Staff Manual respectively. Title Pages will be prepared in manuscript.

WAR DIARY
or
INTELLIGENCE SUMMARY
(Erase heading not required.)

October 1916 U Battery. R.H.A.

Army Form C. 2118.

Place	Date	Hour	Summary of Events and Information	Remarks and references to Appendices
October 1916	20th		VIII 63409 Br. George Eldrington Awarded "Military Medal"	
			For conspicuous ability & gallantry when in command of a detached Signalling Post in the worst of the Hookle barrage. He was 3 times brought to notice by officers of other batteries for running messages when his line was blown to bits and it was entirely due to the stoutheartedness and example that Communication was well maintained between battery and O.P. during very trying 4 days.	
			1/11/16. Riel. Major R.H.A. Cmdg U Bty R.H.A.	

Army Form C. 2118.

Instructions regarding War Diaries and Intelligence Summaries are contained in F. S. Regs., Part II. and the Staff Manual respectively. Title pages will be prepared in manuscript.

WAR DIARY
or
INTELLIGENCE SUMMARY.
(*Erase heading not required.*)

November 1916 — 'U' Battery RHA

Place	Date	Hour	Summary of Events and Information	Remarks and references to Appendices
Crecy.	1st		Packing up to March	
Crecy	2nd		Marched to MOYENNEVILLE Pouring rain. Gen Kavanagh Comdg Cav Corps watched battery march past him. Moyenneville took a bit of getting into as billets were hard to find, but eventually we fitted in very comfortably. Dr Camp to Hosp.	
Moyenneville	3rd		—	
Moyenneville	4th			
Moyenneville	5th			

A5834 Wt. W4973/M687 750,000 8/16 D. D. & L. Ltd. Forms/C.2118/13.

Army Form C. 2118.

WAR DIARY
or
INTELLIGENCE SUMMARY.
(Erase heading not required.)

Instructions regarding War Diaries and Intelligence Summaries are contained in F. S. Regs., Part II. and the Staff Manual respectively. Title pages will be prepared in manuscript.

November 1916 — "U" Battery RHA

Place	Date	Hour	Summary of Events and Information	Remarks and references to Appendices
Moyenneville	6th		Started painting vehicles a shade of light blue with a little grey in it! apparently a very serviceable colour and also looks very nice 41750 Gr Patterson awarded 7 days FP No I.	
Moyenneville	7th.			
Moyenneville	8th.		B.C. went on leave visited Royal Military Academy and got names of cadets to get as Subalterns.	
Moyenneville	9th.			
Moyenneville	10th			
Moyenneville	11th			

A5834 Wt. W4973/M687 750,000 8/16 D. D. & L. Ltd. Forms/C.2118/13.

Army Form C. 2118.

Instructions regarding War Diaries and Intelligence Summaries are contained in F. S. Regs., Part II. and the Staff Manual respectively. Title pages will be prepared in manuscript.

WAR DIARY
or
INTELLIGENCE SUMMARY.
(*Erase heading not required.*)

November 1916 "U" Battery RHA

Place	Date	Hour	Summary of Events and Information	Remarks and references to Appendices
Moyenneville	12th		5 Light Draught Horses arrived from Remount Depot.	
	13th			
	14th			
	15th			
	16th			
	17th			

A5834 Wt. W4973/M687 750,000 8/16 D. D. & L. Ltd. Forms/C.2118/13.

Army Form C. 2118.

WAR DIARY
or
INTELLIGENCE SUMMARY.
(*Erase heading not required.*)

Instructions regarding War Diaries and Intelligence Summaries are contained in F. S. Regs., Part II. and the Staff Manual respectively. Title pages will be prepared in manuscript.

November 1916 — "H" Battery RHA

Place	Date	Hour	Summary of Events and Information	Remarks and references to Appendices
Moyenneville	18th		B.C. returns from leave. Battery Packing up. Gr. Fleming & Oliver to Hosp. Tx. H. W. K. Holmes to 6th Divn.	
Moyenneville	19th		marched to L'ETOILE. 13 miles. Horses in open - very cold. 1 L. D. Horse to M.V.S.	
L'ETOILE	20th		marched to VAUX-EN-AMIENOIS to do depot battery for 4th Army Artillery School. a very poor village. Horses in open, freezing cold. Lt Campbell rejoins Battery.	
VAUX-EN-AMIENOIS	21st		got Horses under cover - no material come for buildings of School or Stables. Started carting chalk for standings	
"	22nd		Chalk Fatigue. Provided a gun carriage for a Coldstreamer who was killed in a trench mortar accident.	
"	23rd		Chalk fatigue. Gr Forsythe G. awarded 14 days F.P. No. I.	

A5834 Wt. W4973/M687 750,000 8/16 D. D. & L. Ltd. Forms/C.2118/13.

Instructions regarding War Diaries and Intelligence Summaries are contained in F. S. Regs., Part II. and the Staff Manual respectively. Title pages will be prepared in manuscript.

WAR DIARY
or
INTELLIGENCE SUMMARY.
(Erase heading not required.)

Army Form C. 2118.

November 1916 — 'L' Battery RHA

Place	Date	Hour	Summary of Events and Information	Remarks and references to Appendices
VAUX.	24th		Chalk fatigues 1 L.D. Horse to M. V. S.	
"	25th		Rain all day so no work done.	
"	26th		Chalk fatigues	
"	27th		"	
"	28th		"	
"	29th		Chalk fatigues redrilling.	
"	30th		" Battery Staff out.	

E Riel
Major RHA
Commanding 'L' Battery RHA.

A5834 Wt. W4973/M687 750,000 8/16 D. D. & L. Ltd. Forms/C.2118/13.

SERIAL NO 273.

Confidential

War Diary

of

"U" Battery, Royal Horse Artillery

FROM 1st. December 1916. TO 31st. December 1916.

For December

Instructions regarding War Diaries and Intelligence Summaries are contained in F. S. Regs., Part II. and the Staff Manual respectively. Title pages will be prepared in manuscript.

WAR DIARY
or
INTELLIGENCE SUMMARY.
(Erase heading not required.)

N Battery RHA 31-12-16

Army Form C. 2118.

Place	Date	Hour	Summary of Events and Information	Remarks and references to Appendices
VAUX-EN-AMIENOIS	1st		Battery Staff Parade	
	2nd		Fatigues for artillery school. Gr. Taylor awarded "Military Medal" for Gallantry at FESTUBERT	
	3rd			
	4th		Drill order Parade	
	5th		Battery Gun Drill. Drs Baker & Clough to Hosp	

A5834 Wt. W4973/M687 750,000 8/16 D. D. & L. Ltd. Forms/C.2118/13.

Instructions regarding War Diaries and Intelligence Summaries are contained in F. S. Regs., Part II. and the Staff Manual respectively. Title pages will be prepared in manuscript.

WAR DIARY
or
INTELLIGENCE SUMMARY.
(Erase heading not required.)

Army Form C. 2118.

December 1916

Place	Date	Hour	Summary of Events and Information	Remarks and references to Appendices
VAUX-EN AMIENOIS	6th		Fatigues Gr Richards to Hosp.	
	7th		Fatigues. Gr Patterson awarded 28 days F.P. No I.	
	8th		Battery Staff Sgt. Gr A.H. Cecil joined from 29th Bde R.F.A.	
	9th		Dr Donaldson awarded 14 days F.P. No I.	
	10th		Played 283 Co R.E. at Football & were beaten. Bdr Creighton to Hosp. 4 Guns & 2 Drs joined from 4th Cav Div Ammn Col. Horse in Bed.	
	11th		Lt Col Rochfort-Boyd D.S.O. R.H.A. Comdg 1st Ind R.H.A. Bde & Major Paymaster 9th Bty R.H.A. came on a visit. G.O.C. 4th Army visited the School.	

A5834 Wt. W4973/M687 750,000 8/16 D. D. & L. Ltd. Forms/C.2118/13.

Instructions regarding War Diaries and Intelligence Summaries are contained in F. S. Regs., Part II. and the Staff Manual respectively. Title pages will be prepared in manuscript.

WAR DIARY
or
INTELLIGENCE SUMMARY.
(Erase heading not required.)

Army Form C. 2118.

December 1916.

Place	Date	Hour	Summary of Events and Information	Remarks and references to Appendices
VAUX EN AMIENOIS	12th		Snow. Gnr Leech to Hosp.	
"	13th		Battery Gun Drill.	
"	14th			
	15th		Bty Staff Parade. Gnrs Whitehead, Randall, Lawsley to Hosp.	
	16th		Gr Fleming rejoined from Hosp.	
	17th		Hockey Match.	

A5834 Wt. W4973/M687 750,000 8/16 D. D. & L. Ltd. Forms/C.2118/13.

Instructions regarding War Diaries and Intelligence Summaries are contained in F. S. Regs., Part II. and the Staff Manual respectively. Title pages will be prepared in manuscript.

WAR DIARY
or
INTELLIGENCE SUMMARY.
(Erase heading not required.)

Army Form C. 2118.

Place	Date	Hour	Summary of Events and Information	Remarks and references to Appendices
VAUX EN AMIENOIS	18th		all N.C.O.s came out jumping over new jumps. Artillery School opened with 20 N.C.O.s Building very backward.	
	19th		Major Rich & B.S.M. Wallis lectured on Interior economy of a Battery. Dr Dutton joined from Hosp.	
	20th		2/Lieut C. G. Darby joined the battery from the Royal Military Academy. School course went out on driving drill. Provided 3 Gun Carriages for funeral of 2 Sergts. killed by Gas fumes from a brazier in enclosed room at the Trench Mortar School.	
	21st		All N.C.O.s out jumping	
	22nd			

Army Form C. 2118.

Instructions regarding War Diaries and Intelligence Summaries are contained in F. S. Regs., Part II. and the Staff Manual respectively. Title pages will be prepared in manuscript.

WAR DIARY
or
INTELLIGENCE SUMMARY.
(Erase heading not required.)

Place	Date	Hour	Summary of Events and Information December 1916	Remarks and references to Appendices
[illegible] AMIENOIS	23rd	5.30 P.M.	Major Reid returned to the Artillery School on Battery Staff.	
	24th		Football match against the R.E. & got beaten [illegible] to [illegible]	
	25th	1 P.M.	Men had Xmas Dinner	
		7 P.M.	The battery entertained the Trench Mortar & Artillery Schools at a concert given in the Gun Park. Sgt Yates assisted by the Q.M.S. Etc gave a splendid entertainment which ended with a play called "The [illegible] Boys are here" written by Sgt Yates and in which an aeroplane came on to the stage. Wigs & costumes were obtained and everyone enjoyed themselves. Refreshments were provided for Everyone.	

A5834 Wt. W4973/M687 750,000 8/16 D. D. & L. Ltd. Forms/C.2118/13.

Instructions regarding War Diaries and Intelligence Summaries are contained in F. S. Regs., Part II. and the Staff Manual respectively. Title pages will be prepared in manuscript.

WAR DIARY
or
INTELLIGENCE SUMMARY.
(Erase heading not required.)

Army Form C. 2118.

Place	Date	Hour	Summary of Events and Information December 1916	Remarks and references to Appendices
VAUX-EN AMIENOIS	26th		Back to fatigues for the School	
	27th			
	28th			
	29th			
	30th		Played NCOs on Course at School at football & beat them	
	31st			

Rich.
Major RHA
Cmdg "L" Battery RHA

A5834 Wt. W4973/M687 750,000 8/16 D. D. & L. Ltd. Forms/C.2118/13.

www.ingramcontent.com/pod-product-compliance
Lightning Source LLC
Chambersburg PA
CBHW081539160426
43191CB00011B/1796